THE CARMELITE WAY

An Ancient Path for Today's Pilgrim

John Welch, O. Carm.

Gracewing.

Gracewing
2 Southern Avenue
Leominster
Herefordshire
HR6 0QF

The Publisher gratefully acknowledges excerpts from the following works. From "Transformed Humanity and St. John of the Cross," in *St. John of the Cross*, by Peter Slattery. Copyright © 1994 by Alba House, New York. From *The Collected Works of St. John of the Cross*, translated by Kieran Kavanaugh and Otilio Rodriguez. Copyright © 1979, 1991 by Washington Province of Discalced Carmelites; ICS Publications, 2131 Lincoln Road, N.E., Washington, D.C. 20002, U.S.A. From *The Collected Works of St. Teresa of Avila, Volume One*, translated by Kieran Kavanaugh and Otilio Rodriguez. Copyright © 1976 by Washington Province of Discalced Carmelites; ICS Publications, 2131 Lincoln Road, N.E., Washington, D.C. 20002, U.S.A. From *The Collected Works of St. Teresa of Avila, Volume Two*, translated by Kieran Kavanaugh and Otilio Rodriguez. Copyright © 1980 by Washington Province of Discalced Carmelites; ICS Publications, 2131 Lincoln Road, N.E., Washington, D.C. 20002, U.S.A. From *The Collected Works of St. Teresa of Avila, Volume Three*, translated by Kieran Kavanaugh and Otilio Rodriguez. Copyright © 1985 by Washington Province of Discalced Carmelites; ICS Publications, 2131 Lincoln Road, N.E., Washington, D.C. 20002, U.S.A. From *Voices, Vision, Smells*, an audiotape by John Welch. Published by Alba House Communications.

Gracewing ISBN 0 85244 311 0

Printed and bound in England by
Antony Rowe Ltd, Eastbourne BN23 6QT

Contents

TO THE CARMELITE FAMILY

Probe me, God, know my heart;
try me, know my thoughts.
See if my way is crooked,
then lead me in the ancient paths.
(Psalm 139)

Introduction

This work attempts to distill recurring themes in the Carmelite tradition. Its purpose is to make available the spiritual wisdom of this eight hundred–year-old religious community.

Carmelites are a Christian religious community born in the early 1200s on Mount Carmel in Palestine. Originally hermits, they soon joined a fast-growing movement in Europe and became one of the mendicant orders of the Middle Ages. Today the lives of Carmelites still blend these eremitical and apostolic roots.

Over the intervening centuries the attempt of the Carmelites to follow Christ has woven a large and colorful historical tapestry. Most Carmelites are relatively unknown to history, including the first Carmelites. But some have become revered figures whose determined search for God has become an inspiration for countless others. Among these are Peter Thomas, Andrew Corsini, Mary Magdalene de' Pazzi, Teresa of Avila, John of the Cross, John of St.-Samson, Elizabeth of the Trinity, Thérèse of Lisieux, Titus Brandsma, and Edith Stein.

A tradition of spirituality is like an ancient path. It is shaped over the course of time and well-worn by travelers. People continue to take the path because it has proven to be reliable. Today's traveler trusts its contours because of others' testimony.

The Carmelite tradition is just such an ancient path. The first tracings of the path were begun by a practically anonymous band of men in a wadi, a canyon on Mount Carmel. But slowly, as pilgrims found it a way which aided their journey, the original faint traces deepened, widened, and the path became more distinct and sure. It can now be found on most maps which chart regions of the soul.

A Christian spiritual tradition is a telling of the gospel through the images and language of a particular group of

Christians. Their telling of the story is shaped over time as they attempt to respond to the challenges of the gospel. They eventually find their own expressive way of giving an account of the paschal mystery, the dying and rising of Christ, present in their own lives.

Each tradition establishes an atmosphere. The words, the images, the history and the biographies of the community, all create a spiritual environment for the seeker. A tradition develops a soul language. It creates a land where God's spirit and the human spirit may meet.

This meeting with God takes place in our human experience. A religious tradition provides a horizon within which our ordinary experience is opened to its spiritual depths. In this way a tradition mediates the transcendent and allows us to attend to God's presence and call. The tradition also provides a particular language for interpreting and communicating our experience of God.

The Carmelite tradition tells the story of God's presence to us through images and language which are particularly, but not exclusively, Carmelite. Over their long history Carmelites have shown a preference for certain images and themes from the Christian tradition; they have also drawn from their own imagination to add to the Christian thesaurus.

The Carmelite telling of the story cannot be anything more than, nor should it be anything less than, the Christ story of the gospels. It is the gospel told in the language of a particular community of Christians called Carmelites.

A pilgrim has expectations of a tradition. It should be able to offer a compelling Christian vision for life's journey. It should identify a goal, and warn of difficulties and problems to be encountered on the way. It must provide a map for traveling the way, and offer resources for overcoming its difficulties. A tradition also needs to be able to tell a story of victory over apparent defeat, and celebrate, in anticipation, a goal not yet reached.

Such expectations structure this present work. This interpretation of the Carmelite tradition is *one* Carmelite's perspective. Any one perspective will necessarily be uneven. The principal sources for this work are the documents and history of the early Carmelites, and the writings of the sixteenth-century Carmelite mystics, Teresa of Avila and John of the Cross. While other Carmelite figures are included in the work, Teresa and John remain the best exponents of the Carmelite tradition.

Chapter One

THE VISION OF THE CARMELITES

Beginnings of the Carmelite Tradition and Efforts to Renew

It is one matter to have a vision of life's possibilities; it is another to give it concrete shape, and it is a third matter to sustain the vision. This process is necessary whether for an individual or a community. The longer the vision must be sustained the greater the possibility of it becoming dimmed, and, concomitantly, the greater the need to renew and reinvigorate the original vision.

The Christian community calling itself Carmelite has attempted to sustain a vision for almost eight hundred years. The fact that the vision still energizes and challenges people is testimony to its power. But it is a vision necessarily incarnated in human beings whose faithfulness to the vision suffers the vagaries of human existence. In other words, the Carmelites have frequently let themselves and others down, and have had to remorsefully pick themselves up. The history of the Carmelites, from one perspective, is a lesson about the danger of human hubris and the consequences of neglecting essential values; it is also a testimony to the human spirit, which has the capability of going once more to the well of its imagination and drawing up an image of what once was and what still could be.

"Nor is it in any way good," wrote the Carmelite Teresa of Avila, "for persons to complain if they see their order in some decline; rather, they should strive to be the kind of rock on which the edifice may again be raised, for the Lord will help toward that."[1] The story of Carmel is the story of just such people stepping forward, time and again, to call others to a renewal of the original vision, at the same time reminding them of their own deepest desires.

The following is a brief account of the beginnings of this community, and succeeding efforts by Carmelite men and women to take responsibility for their order and its vision.

The First Carmelites

The path of Carmel begins in a place of attentiveness to God, a mountainous ridge jutting out into the Mediterranean Sea. Mount Carmel forms the southern boundary of the bay of Haifa in Israel. Here between heaven and earth, sea and land, people gathered in prayer, among them the prophet Elijah. He would be identified with the path which would be Carmel.

In the late twelfth century C.E. the original Carmelites gathered on the mountain and in its canyons in order to escape their former lives, to be free of the pressures and expectations which imprisoned them, and to set straight their priorities. Probably most were from other countries, choosing to begin again in an unknown land.

They were from the west, Latins, living in a crusader-protected area called the Kingdom of Jerusalem, or the Latin Kingdom. Under the crusaders, all of Palestine was known as the Kingdom of Jerusalem. But Saladin, at the battle of Hattin in 1187, defeated the crusaders and restored most of the land to Muslim control. Richard the Lionheart recaptured Acre in 1191 and entered into a treaty which gave the crusaders control over a thin strip of land on the coast of Palestine, the remnant of the Kingdom of Jerusalem. This coastal land included Mount Carmel. It is most probable that the first Carmelites began living on Mount Carmel sometime after this period. Perhaps some of the hermits were from other eremitical locations in Palestine and Antioch, now untenable.[2]

The original Carmelites settled on Mount Carmel by a spring known as "the fountain of Elijah." The spring was at the opening of the wadi 'ain es-Siah which was approximately two kilometers inland from the point of the promontory. The wadi ran about a thousand meters east and west, opening to the Mediterranean. Here Carmelites lived for the first one hundred years of their existence.

These men left almost nothing in the way of written records. When history first took notice of them they were already a functioning community. Early in the 1200s, sightings of the Carmelites began to appear in reports of pilgrims on their way to Jerusalem. Pilgrims landed north of Mount Carmel at Acre and traveled south along the coast on the *via maris*, passing the location of the fountain of Elijah. Even at this early date the pilgrims were able to report that the church visible in the wadi was dedicated to the Virgin Mary.

Jacques de Vitry, who was bishop of Acre from 1216 to 1228, also left a testimony to their existence. Identifying locations in Palestine where the eremitical life flourished, he observed: "...others after the example and in imitation of holy solitary Elijah the prophet lived as hermits in the beehives of small cells on Mount Carmel...near the spring which is called the Spring of Elijah."[3]

The earliest recorded communication from the Carmelites themselves has been preserved in the opening lines of their constitutions of 1281. These lines, identified as the *Rubrica Prima*, quite possibly date back to the 1230s when some of the Carmelites had begun migrating back to Europe and their identity was in question. This response was to be given by members of the order when questioned about their heritage:

> We declare, bearing testimony to the truth, that from the time when the prophets Elijah and Elisha dwelt devoutly on Mount Carmel, holy Fathers both of the Old and the New Testament, whom the contemplation of heavenly things drew to the solitude of the same mountain, have without doubt led praiseworthy lives there by the fountain of Elijah in holy penitence unceasingly and successfully maintained.

> It was these same successors whom Albert the patriarch of Jerusalem in the time of Innocent III united into a community, writing a rule for them which Pope Honorius, the successor of the same Innocent, and many of their successors, approving this Order, most devoutly confirmed by their charters. In the profession of this rule, we, their followers, serve the Lord in diverse parts of the world, even to the present day.[4]

These first Carmelites were men who must have had a conversion in their life, a serious change of lifestyle and a reordering of their values. As part of their conversion they went apart in solitude leaving traditional roles in society. And they were pilgrims, people whose conversion took them to the periphery of society and the church to live on the patrimony of Jesus Christ and there serve their liege Lord.

We do not know the names of these first Carmelites.[5] But we do know their hearts. From the beginning this tradition rooted itself in the deep hungers of the human heart. These men could only have located themselves on this mountain and begun a life together in response to such hungers, such "deep caverns of feeling," later captured in the poetry of John of the Cross. Why else live where they lived?

We can assume they had tried to feed these hungers with the normal food which nourishes life: relationships, possessions, plans, titles, reputations. They probably found that their efforts and their control brought little peace to their lives. They had not found food sufficient to feed their hunger.

And so they laid their lives down and began again. Perhaps they were escaping more than simply restlessness. Perhaps lives had come apart in deep disappointment; perhaps they experienced unbearable losses; perhaps they were chased from other places, or even were escaping the law.

But it was more than escape that brought them to Mount Carmel. They assembled there because of a call. I would think they were people who were haunted in some ways and who found one another on a mountain which evoked their desires. People today come to this tradition because they, too, experience themselves as pilgrims on this earth, having deep hungers, and haunted by a call.

The conditions on Mount Carmel are inviting. The site slopes to the waters of the Mediterranean. Its breezes cool the canyon. Within its walls the men lived at slight distances from one another, spending time in reflection and prayer. They read scripture and carried its lines in their hearts. They fasted, abstained from meat, and worked in silence. They gathered regularly: daily for mass, weekly for discussions. They lived a life of poverty, and what they owned they owned together. Their leader was elected and he was to live at the entrance to the site. Life on Mount Carmel focused their scattered lives, and settled their confused minds. It freed hearts that had been anxious about many things. The oratory in the midst of the cells invited them to find a center in the midst of their lives.

These elements were collected into a brief formula of life which became the Rule of the Carmelites. Albert, the Patriarch of Jerusalem who was living in Acre, gave this formula of life to the community sometime between 1206 and 1214. He concluded the document with an admonition: "Here then are a few points I have written down to provide you with a standard of conduct to live up to....See that the bond of common sense is the guide of the virtues."[6] While not specifically mentioned in the Rule, there are indications that the hermits on Mount Carmel engaged in some pastoral activity. Such activity would not have been incongruent with the eremitical life.

As early as 1238 Carmelites began to leave Mount Carmel for new sites in Europe. By 1291, after an existence of approximately one hundred years in the canyon, all Carmelites had withdrawn. Muslim and Christian warfare made the mountain untenable. "The inroads of the pagans," wrote Pope Innocent IV, "have driven our beloved sons, the hermits of Mount Carmel, to betake themselves, not without great affliction of spirit, to parts across the sea."[7]

They traveled to Cyprus, Sicily, France, and England. Initially they intended to continue an eremitical existence, but very quickly they were transformed into one of the mendicant orders, taking their place with the Franciscans, Dominicans, and Augustinians.

Their formula of life given by Albert changed into its final form in 1247 and became the official Rule of the Carmelites. The change strengthened their common life and allowed them to live, not only in solitude, but also where it was convenient for their way of life.[8]

The development of the order took place over a vast geographical panorama. By the end of the thirteenth century, sixty years after arriving in Europe, the order had grown from a small band of men in a narrow valley in Palestine to about 150 houses, divided into twelve provinces throughout Europe and the Mediterranean. With practically no official documentation of its beginnings, except for its Rule and constitutions, with no founder, and with an anonymous first community, Carmel closed the thirteenth century with its first doctorates in theology. Gerard of Bologna received his doctorate from the University of Paris in 1295. Two years later he was elected Prior General of the order.

The brief time on Mount Carmel forevermore shaped the ancient path of the Carmelite tradition. Each major figure on the path of Carmel returned to the mountain in memory and in heart to be renewed by the original impulses which gathered the group in cells and around the oratory. Perhaps, too, each person read back into the beginnings what he or she needed to find. For example, John of Hildesheim (d. 1375) evoked their memory, but with some romanticism: "The primitive dwellers on Mount Carmel were simple hermits, unlettered, poor, they possessed no parchments, nor were they writers. They were accustomed to pray rather than to write."[9]

Later travelers of the ancient path continued to mine the mountain, going deeper into the themes and implications of that long-ago existence. When Teresa of Avila began her reformed convents of Carmelite nuns she had as a blueprint in her mind the original Carmelite setting on Mount Carmel. Earlier reforms, as well, attempted to return to the original vision.

Decline, the Reform of Mantua, and John Soreth

In the fourteenth century Carmel produced the outstanding figures of St. Andrew Corsini and St. Peter Thomas. Andrew

Corsini (d. 1374), from Florence, received a doctorate in theology from the University of Paris, was elected provincial, and then appointed Bishop of Fiesole. He was known for the simplicity of his life, his care of the poor, and his excellent preaching. Peter Thomas (d. 1366), from Aquitaine, became an advisor to Avignon popes and was sent on numerous diplomatic missions for the papacy, including missions to Serbia and Constantinople for the promotion of church unity. He was appointed archbishop of Crete and Patriarch of Constantinople.

However, the fervor of the order began to wane in the late fourteenth century and the malaise grew worse in the fifteenth century. Religious life slowly entered a period of decline everywhere. The general population of Europe was decimated by a plague, the Black Death, in the years 1348 and 1349. It is not known how badly the disease affected the order directly, but it is known that during a General Chapter in Metz in 1348, two hundred friars died, either during the sessions, or traveling to or from the sessions. The Hundred Years War was another type of plague which affected religious life. During this warfare between England and France (1337–1453) about thirty of the ninety Carmelite houses in France were destroyed, either through fighting or for use in building defenses.

In 1432, Eugene IV modified the Rule of Carmel. This "second mitigation" allowed the friars, on suitable occasions, to remain and walk about in their churches and cloisters and their periphery, and to eat meat three times a week. Later legislation reduced abstinence days to Wednesday, Friday, and Saturday. Although not written into the official text of the Rule, this second mitigation concluded the process of the hermits on Mount Carmel gaining mendicant status. Actually, the mitigation merely ratified the lifestyle already prevalent. However, to many people, these changes were an indication of a gradual loss of Carmel's original vision and spirit. Later reformers, including Teresa of Avila, often rejected this mitigation.

Blessed John Soreth (c. 1395–1471), who had received a doctorate from the University of Paris in 1438, was elected Prior General of the order in 1451. A reform-minded general, Soreth nonetheless defended the changes in the Rule. Movement about the churches and cloisters was a fact and a necessity and did not necessarily undermine the prescription to remain in or near one's cell. He wrote:

> To remove the scruples of the weak, this has been declared by Eugene IV to mean that it is permitted to remain and freely walk about in churches, cloisters and precincts of convents, meditating on the law of the Lord, or praying, and serving in proper occupations.

He also defended changes in the abstinence prescriptions:

> Our mendicant state does not possess streams nor sources whence fish for the nourishment of the brethren may be obtained...Our Father Basil says in his rule that those foods must by all means be used that can be more easily and cheaply obtained; but in many places meat is of this kind. Therefore out of a sort of pressing need we poor friars are obliged sometimes to eat it, lest on account of abstinence we be found to seek after food of a more expensive kind and difficult to obtain."[10]

Although he defended the changes, John Soreth was well aware of the unhealthy state of the order. "The Rule and institutions of the Order now lie everywhere neglected. Who keeps them, or who knows them?"[11] he complained. The decline of religious life was marked by an absence of a vital prayer life, serious lapses in the practice of poverty, and a general disregard for the common life.

A reform had already begun early in the fifteenth century when LaSelve, a community located between Florence and Pisa declared itself a "house of observance." It was joined by another community in Mantua. Soon these houses and others who joined them became a distinct entity in the order, the Mantuan reform, and were placed directly under the jurisdiction of the general.

The Mantuan reform stressed silence and a cloister, forbidding entrance to outsiders. The friars were not allowed to be aimlessly outside the convent. Money was distributed from a common chest and the reformers rejected the mitigation of the Rule which allowed them to include meat in their diet three times a week.

A leading reform figure, Blessed Baptist of Mantua, explained, "The Mantua Congregation rising at the inspiration of God from the sordid neglect into which practically the whole Order had fallen, strives to pattern its life and customs after the ancient Fathers."[12] The reform grew under the generalate of John Soreth. By the time of the death of Baptist of Mantua the congregation had thirty-one houses of friars and seven houses of nuns.

Carmelite Sisters

As part of the renewal of the order, John Soreth encouraged the establishment of communities of Carmelite women. The Carmelites had been exempted from responsibility for women's communities in 1261.[13] But in 1452 a papal Bull, *Cum Nulla*, gave Carmelites the authorization to affiliate women's communities with the order. The first communities of Carmelite women, formally constituted, were in Guelders in the Netherlands, and in Florence. Another early example, initiated under Soreth, was the incorporation of a community of nuns established by Frances D'Amboise in 1460. D'Amboise, who received the habit from Soreth, reminds one of a later Carmelite nun, Teresa of Avila, when she says, "The Rule is not longer for one than for another.... To consider and be concerned with who is the grandest lady and comes from the noblest and richest family is the doctrine of the devil."[14] The communities of nuns established by Soreth were cloistered.

John Soreth never visited Spain, and consequently communities there developed differently, but most began after *Cum Nulla*. The Incarnation in Avila, founded in 1479, was the earliest Carmelite women's community in Castile. The Carmelite provincial gave the habit to Doña Elvira Gonzalez who became the first superior. In 1513 the Incarnation moved to bigger quarters outside the city. In 1535 Teresa de Ahumada, to be known as St. Teresa of Avila, entered the Incarnation.

The Reform of Albi

Hearing of the Mantuan reform, the Bishop of Albi in Aquitaine, France, contacted members of the reform in northern Italy and invited friars to come to his diocese and reform the Carmelites. He had previously reformed the Franciscans and Dominicans. When only one friar returned as a candidate for the reform, the bishop sought vocations at the University of Paris. Twenty-six candidates responded, twenty-two of whom would eventually enter the order. They lived in the bishop's palace for a month, receiving instruction in the Carmelite life. The twenty-two received the habit of Carmel in the episcopal palace. The bishop then invited the local community of Carmelites to dinner. While the convent was deserted, the novices and the novice master entered and took possession. The former community were compelled either to join the reform of Albi or go to other communities.

Just as the Mantuan congregation became a separate congregation within the order under a vicar-general, so too the Congregation of Albi received special status. Baptist of Mantua, previously vicar of the Mantuan congregation, had been elected general of the entire order. He warmly welcomed this new reform effort. He wrote:

> As from the beginning, I recall, I favored your congregation, when at the request of the Lord Bishop of Albi, I sent Friar Eligius, said to be still living, so ever since I have with a view to your advantage always favored it, favor it now and will continue to favor it, as long as God grants me life. I praise, approve and commend the privileges which his Holiness our Lord the Pope has granted you and your congregation. I exhort you never to abandon your proposal of leading a holy life, but to adhere to it more strongly and constantly day by day. By so doing you will win salvation for yourselves; for those who have set out down the wide road you will provide an incentive for reconsideration and for recalling and pondering the meaning of their vows.[15]

As with the Mantuan reform, the reform of Albi produced many holy men. The Albi congregation, because it eventually included the student house at the University of Paris, also counted a number of the scholars of the order. Neither reform impacted the entire order.

The principal area of renewal in the order was north of the Alps where John Soreth had long labored. His renewal of Carmel included a restoration of the common life, a renunciation of possessions, a commitment to a contemplative life, and careful observance of the Rule, constitutions, and liturgies of the order.

Soreth's reforms did not spread to Spain, nor did he or any other general visit Spain in the fifteenth century. An early sixteenth-century report on the Carmelite Castilian houses of Toledo, Avila, and San Pablo de la Moraleja judged them to be in deplorable condition, with a number of the friars giving public scandal. Matters were probably not much better in other Spanish Carmelite communities. The crown became involved in religious life renewal, and after the Council of Trent, when reform was introduced into the entire church, the often difficult relationships among Rome, the crown, and order authorities added to the difficulties of renewal.

Nicholas Audet and a Program of Renewal

In 1523 a major program for renewal of the order was published by Nicholas Audet, former provincial of the Holy Land and now vicar-general of the order. Audet was one of the great generals of the order who labored for thirty years to renew the spirit of Carmel. He was appointed by Pope Adrian VI and confirmed by Pope Clement VII with the authority to visit and reform communities in the order. After consulting with princes and prelates before taking up his task, Audet expressed concern at the situation of the order:

> From frequent conversations with them we learned of what sordid conduct many of our brethren are guilty

> and what a great threat hangs over the good because of their bad example, unless all of us together quickly come to our senses and reform our conduct....We are threatened unless we quickly confront and immediately provide a remedy for a number of wrong and wicked deeds committed in our Order.[16]

Audet's program for beginning a reform was titled *Isagogicon* and it included a number of specific prescriptions, among them:

> Within three days of receipt of the prescriptions, each friar is to hand to the prior a list of all his possessions. It is emphasized that what they have is not their own but for their use.
>
> Specific academic disciplines are recommended for the various levels of formation of candidates and further training is recommended, including university training, to raise the intellectual level of the Order.
>
> No one is to live outside a house of the Order; anyone outside the Order is to return.
>
> Sermons are to be given on all Sundays and feast days and each day in Lent.
>
> Superiors are to receive only legitimate income and must cease selling certain privileges such as the office of prior, academic degrees, and permissions to live outside the Order.
>
> Detailed prescriptions are to be followed for liturgical services and presence in choir.
>
> Friars are allowed to leave the house only twice a week, in pairs, and with white mantles. Few lay men are to be admitted into the house, and no women, except those of the nobility who cannot be refused entrance.

> Professed students are to follow detailed instructions regarding studies and behavior. When playing sports they must wear their habits.
>
> All are to eat in the refectory; silence is the norm and there is to be reading from the Bible or other suitable book. No bread and wine may be taken to one's room.[17]

With this program, additional reform decrees from the general chapter, and a revised version of Soreth's Constitutions, Audet began a visitation of provinces, beginning in Italy, in an attempt to carry out the necessary reforms. The turmoil of the Protestant Reformation added to his difficulties, especially in countries where reform efforts might prove effective. Audet spent three years in France and Germany and managed to introduce reforms in more than one hundred houses. A number of men left the order under pressure to reform. In the Spanish province of Castile, more than half the friars walked away.

In 1553 Pope Julius III ordered the development of a plan for the renewal of religious life. The text of the Bull was submitted to certain superiors for comment, and Audet's comments have been preserved. His supportive, tactful, moderate suggestions show the wisdom gained in his years of struggle to call the order to a faithful following of its original impetus. By the time he died in 1562, a movement had begun in Spain which, had he known about it, would have received his full support. As it was, his successor, John Rossi, gave quick encouragement to this burgeoning reform effort beginning in Castile.

The Reform of Teresa of Avila

In sixteenth-century Spain, at the age of forty-seven, and after living twenty-seven years in the Carmelite convent of the Incarnation in Avila, Teresa de Ahumada gave fresh impetus to the tradition of Carmel. Dissatisfied with the size and atmosphere of the Incarnation, she envisioned small communities of women whose prayer would further the work of the church. These groups of women were to be friends with God and friends with one another.

In her time in the Incarnation the community had grown to more than 140 solemnly professed nuns. During one period of time more than fifty were living outside the convent, in part because of the difficulty in feeding so many. The Incarnation had a cloister, but it was easily entered by relatives, servants, and young girls for education. Many of the nuns had their own patrimony. Nuns who were of the nobility might have suites with kitchens, as did Teresa who was a doña; poorer nuns lived in dormitories. Singing the divine office took up much of the day. All things considered, the Incarnation was an observant community, but crowded. In too many ways it was entangled with, and mirrored, the surrounding society.

Teresa had a high regard for many of the women in the Incarnation. Later, when others were complaining that Teresa's reform was draining the Incarnation of its best members, she replied that there were more than forty left who could be foundresses themselves.[18]

Remembering the beginnings of the order on Mount Carmel, Teresa wanted to reestablish the eremitical conditions which prevailed in the wadi. She wanted her nuns to understand themselves as solitaries in community. They were to follow the primitive Rule of Carmel, meaning the Rule of 1247, which she understood was "without mitigation."[19]

The atmosphere of the houses of Teresa's reform was to be conducive to an attentiveness to God. The quiet of the caves and huts on Mount Carmel permeated the rooms and corridors of the new Carmels. Teresa encouraged the women to speak trustingly with Christ, as though with a friend. They could imagine their friend beside them, or within them, especially in gospel settings where he is alone and might appreciate company. Hermitages were established within the convent gardens for times of greater solitude.

But they were also to take time to be present to one another and nurture loving relationships. If you want to know God, she wrote, know God's friends. Initially, Teresa allowed no more than thirteen women in each community, a number allowing for levels of relationships, with the possibility of each woman being known at some depth by every other woman. Teresa set a clear, but challenging, goal: "all must be friends, all must be loved, all must be held dear, all must be helped."[20] As friends they recreated, prayed the psalms in chapel, and attended celebrations of the eucharist.

As with the men who were drawn to Mount Carmel, Teresa's women were looking for conditions which would provide a setting, a structure, a support for attending to the mystery which haunted their lives and made them restless and unsatisfied with other forms of living. Teresa herself said, "I wanted to live (for I well understood that I was not living but was struggling with a shadow of death), but I had no one to give me life, and I was unable to catch hold of it."[21] For many of the women, to enter such a community was like coming home. "It seemed to me," wrote Anne of St. Bartholomew, one of the first members, "that from my earliest childhood until this, I had lived this kind of a life and had dwelt among these saints."[22]

When Teresa made her first foundation in 1562, John Rossi was vicar-general of the order. The next year the Council of Trent ended and Rossi had the task of visiting, correcting, and reforming the houses of the order. In 1564 Rossi was elected general and the Counter-Reformation and implementation of the decrees of Trent began. Rossi was appreciative and supportive of Teresa's efforts to renew the order. When he died, Teresa expressed deep sorrow.

Teresa would eventually create an inner space to complement the outer space of her convents. In *The Interior Castle* she imagined the soul as a castle, and life's journey was through the various rooms of the castle to a central room where the king lived. The king, almost imperceptibly at first, invites those wandering outside the castle walls to enter within and join him in a loving union. Teresa's new communities were to be the settings for this interior journey. But she needed allies in her reform.

John of the Cross

Juan de Yepes was restless in his new life with the Carmelites. He had recently completed his novitiate in the order and was now a student of theology at the University of Salamanca. But he wanted something more—or something else. He was considering joining the Carthusians. Obviously, whatever his dissatisfactions were, they had something to do with the deeper hungers of his heart and the conditions in which these could be nourished.

Just at that point in his life, he was introduced to Teresa of Avila, who was busy beginning the second house of her reform in John's hometown of Medina del Campo. Teresa was older than John by twenty-seven years, but she saw in this little friar the person she was seeking to begin her reform among the male Carmelites. John immediately resonated with Teresa's vision, and volunteered to join her movement after he had completed his last year of studies, but only if she moved quickly on the project.

One year later Teresa put John through a short, second novitiate with her, introducing him to the spirit of her reformed communities. He then began his own community with two other friars in an isolated place called Duruelo. Their seriousness could be seen in the skulls and crosses which decorated the house; their asceticism was evident as the snow came through the cracks of the building and they walked barefoot about the house and the countryside. The blueprint of the first Carmelites on Mount Carmel guided a new expression in sixteenth-century Spain.

When Teresa was assigned back to her original convent of the Incarnation to bring about its reform, she requested John of the Cross as chaplain for the nuns. And so, for a period of two years, until Teresa completed her term as prioress, these two extraordinary people ministered in the same community.

But tensions were growing within the order as a result of the reform efforts. Differing visions and competing authorities led to deep divisions. John of the Cross suffered for his close identification with the reform movement. He was forcibly removed from the Incarnation and taken to a monastery prison cell in Toledo. There, in the dark of his nine-month confinement, John began to compose the mystical poetry which was an expression of his experience of God's love. Later, after he had escaped, John continued writing poetry and also prose commentaries on his poems.

John was a specialist in analyzing the desires of the human heart. He spoke of our desires as always being restless and our hearts endlessly searching. John likened our desires to little children who only momentarily quiet down, but soon erupt again; or like the situation of a lover who waits expectantly for a day with a loved one, only to have the day be a great disappointment. "Where have you hidden, beloved?" he wrote. "I went out calling you, but you were gone."[23]

John's conclusion was that human beings have a desire or yearning which nothing in this world can ultimately satisfy. In John's experience only that mysterious Presence dwelling at the center of each one's life is sufficient food for the hungers of the heart. John imaged this Mystery as a night, a flame, a lover. "The soul's center is God," he concluded.[24]

The Reform of Touraine

The reform inspired by Teresa and John eventually became an order itself, the Discalced Carmelites. In the next century, in France, three men would converge whose spirit provided the impetus which would eventually contribute to the reform of the entire Carmelite order. Peter Behourt had joined the order in 1582, the year Teresa of Avila died. His intent was clear: "From the time I entered the order, I have always chosen, desired, and hoped for the restoration to a better state of the whole province."[25] He continually attempted to recruit others to become a core of reform. His efforts in a series of offices in several communities resulted in mixed outcomes. His was not the personality to rally men for a sustained living of a more disciplined life.

But a similar movement in the house of studies in Paris, the Place Maubert, took on life. There, Philip Thibault stood out as a leader. He was acquainted with Pierre Berulle and was influenced by the spiritual movements associated with the salon of Madame Acarie. Thibault and several students made a pilgrimage to Rome in 1600 to ask church and order leaders to allow them a separate existence within the order, or to join the Discalced. They were persuaded to remain in the order and work for its reform.

Thibault joined Behourt and a small community at Rennes. He was to be sub-prior and novice master. The friars renewed their profession, bound themselves to an effort at reform, and mandated a second novitiate for all who joined the reform. The Observance of Rennes had begun. Eventually Thibault became prior, and to the reform he contributed the new forms of prayer then current in French spirituality.

Joining the community in Rennes in 1612 was a lay brother, John of St.-Samson. John was blind from the age of three, an orphan at ten, and a devout, prayerful searching soul who had been living in Paris with a grocer near the Carmelite house in Place Maubert. He spent long hours of prayer in the church. John was musically gifted and on one occasion asked one of the friars if he could play the church organ.[26] John eventually was given a room in the convent in recompense for playing the organ and giving lessons. He became part of a study group in the house and listened to spiritual texts read aloud.

John entered the Carmelite novitiate at Dol, just as the community fled because of a plague. John remained to nurse the other novice who had become ill. Eventually John contracted the disease and had to recover at a sanatorium. At age forty-one he entered the reform community of Rennes, joining Behourt and Thibault, made the prescribed second novitiate, and remained at Rennes for the rest of his life. He became unofficial spiritual director for generations of novices and professed students. He was also esteemed and visited by many well-known people of the day who came to talk to the blind mystic of Carmel.[27]

The Observance of Rennes spread to other houses and became the Reform of Touraine. It was a reform which took inspiration, in part, from Teresa and the Discalced Carmelites. The Italian Discalced Congregation's Constitutions of 1611 were available to members of the reform as a model of legislation which was also a spiritual document. The contemplative nature of Carmel was emphasized by the statutes of the Touraine reform as they encouraged "the practice of divine contemplation and the love of holy solitude, formerly the only part of our sacred Order, now its principal part." Again, "for our Carmelite forefathers dwelling in deserts and solitude one thing was necessary: to attend upon *(vacare)* God by the continual exercise of contemplation." But since they were now also called by the church to active ministry, "the nature of our institute requires that to mystical theology, which is the best part for Carmelites, we should add the assiduous study of letters and the sciences."[28] The Reform of Touraine was part of an order-wide movement of the Stricter Observance. Eventually Touraine's statutes were the basis for reform throughout the Carmelite order, influencing legislation into the twentieth century.

The Carmelite Witness

The renewal of a life begins deep down in the heart. Individuals are often alone in pulling their lives together and beginning again. Often, the reform of a community depends, similarly, on just one person's desire for change. Their spark is joined quickly by similar embers in the hearts of others.

Most efforts at reform die. Some are misguided, some lack the soil to take root, some are concretized in structures which humanly are unsustainable. Given the history of Carmel, it is remarkable that the fragile life woven in a wadi on Mount Carmel has not been completely unraveled by the vicissitudes of history and human fickleness. That Carmel exists today could be interpreted as a result of the Spirit moving over chaotic waters; human inconsistency and sinfulness answered by divine faithfulness.

Carmel learned to tell the story of the human heart as a love story. Thinking they were searching for something missing in their lives, Carmelites discovered they were being pursued by a loving Presence whose desire for them gave them increased life, greater freedom, and a trustworthy relationship for their guidance.

The core value at all times in Carmelite history has been that mysterious Presence met deep within searching lives. Carmelites have left a trail of structures and literature born out of engagement with that Presence. The ways of organizing Carmel's life have been multiple: an orderly, eremitical life in a canyon on the mountainous ridge of Carmel; later, a community of men living in the midst of people and serving their needs; still later, communities of women, cloistered and active, in the service of the church; and always, individuals who go even farther apart in the solitude of hermitages.

The external structures are meant to assist an internal journey which Carmel's literature has imaged in various ways: among them, a journey through a castle, traveling a "little way," a passage through a dark night, a search for the beloved in mountain pastures. The last image recalling where it all began.

NOTES

1. Teresa of Avila, *The Foundations*, in *The Collected Works of St. Teresa of Avila*, 3, trans. Kieran Kavanaugh, O.C.D., and Otilio Rodriguez, O.C.D. (Washington, D.C.: ICS Publications, 1985), chap. 4, par. 7.

2. Joachim Smet, O. Carm., *The Carmelites*, 1 (Darien, IL: Carmelite Spiritual Center, 1988), 5.

3. Carlo Cicconetti, O. Carm., *The Rule of Carmel*, trans. Gabriel Pausback, O. Carm., ed. Paul Hoban, O. Carm. (Darien, IL: Carmelite Spiritual Center, 1984), 62.

4. Smet, 15, 16. The original Latin text may be found in Adrianus Staring, O. Carm., *Medieval Carmelite Heritage* (Rome: Institutum Carmelitanum, 1989), 40, 41.

5. See Elias Friedman, *The Latin Hermits of Mount Carmel* (Roma: Institutum Historicum Teresianum, 1979), 189–193. Of the first generation of Carmelites who actually lived on Mount Carmel, only three names are known for certain: Dominic and James, witnesses to a will in Acre in 1273, and William of Sanvico who was definitor from the Holy Land at the general chapter of 1287.

6. See *Albert's Way*, ed. Michael Mulhall, O. Carm. (Rome: Institutum Carmelitanum, 1989). The text of the Rule can be found on pages 2–21. An English translation of the Rule is in the Appendix of this present work.

Albert was chosen Patriarch of Jerusalem in 1205. Arriving in the Holy Land he settled his See at Acre during the first months of 1206. Before his election as Patriarch he was Bishop of Bobbio in 1184 and of Vercelli from 1185 until 1205. During that time he had been delegated by Pope Innocent III to develop a "form of life" for the Humiliati, a group of workers who had several conflicts with the hierarchy. It was a movement comprised of clerics and lay celibates as well as some married people. Albert became both Patriarch of Jerusalem and Papal Legate to the Holy Land. He was given the task of reintegrating the Holy Land.

7. Smet, 10.

8. The Rule of 1247 shows a strengthening of comunity life and a movement to towns as the Carmelites took on a mendicant status. It does not set up an opposition between a contemplative life and ministry since these new mendicants would have understood themselves as contemplatives as well. Probably a predominantly lay group in the beginning, the Carmelites quickly became more clerical.

9. Smet, 50.

10. Ibid., 73.

11. Ibid., 67.

12. Ibid., 76.

13. Women and lay men had been associated with the order in one form or another from early times. Records show that in 1284 lay people affiliated with the order through vows of some type. In 1304 a woman made a profession in Bologna. In 1343 a husband and wife made vows in Florence, vows which seem to be identical to the vows of the friars. Joan of Toulouse is an early fifteenth-century example of a woman associated with the order living as an anchoress. See Smet, 88.

14. Smet, 95.

15. Ibid., 110, 111.

16. Ibid., 155.

17. For further details see Smet, 155–158.

18. For a description of the problems of the Incarnation see Kieran Kavanaugh's introduction to St. Teresa of Avila's *The Foundations* in *The Collected Works*, 19, 20.

19. Knowledge of the Rule would have been part of Teresa's formation. But it is not known if she had access to a copy of the Rule. A manuscript rather recently discovered seems to have belonged to the Incarnation. It has three versions of the Rule, but in poor Spanish.

Neither Albert's formula of life nor the final 1247 text of Innocent IV forbids owning property in common and having fixed income. But a papal decree in 1229 forbade the ownership of common property and possessions. When Teresa was informed of this understanding of the Rule she decided to found her communities, "in poverty," without endowment.

By the time of the first foundation of St. Joseph's in Avila Teresa had a copy of the Rule and it appears to have been, along with customs, the only legislation for the new foundation. The text of the Rule in St. Joseph's was identical to the text used at the Incarnation, since the mitigations after 1247 were not written into the text of the Rule. Insisting that the Rule and Constitutions be read together, Teresa was instrumental in having published the first printed edition of the Rule in Spanish. See *Saint Teresa and the Carmelite Rule* (Roma: Casa Generalizia Carmelitani Scalzi, 1994).

20. *The Way of Perfection*, in *The Collected Works of St. Teresa of Avila*, 2, chap. 4, no. 7.

21. *Life*, in *The Collected Works of St. Teresa*, chap. 8, no. 12.

22. *Autobiography of the Blessed Mother Anne of Saint Bartholomew* (St. Louis, MO: Translated from French by a religious of the Carmel of St. Louis, 1916), 17.

23. John of the Cross, "The Spiritual Canticle," in *The Collected Works of St. John of the Cross*, trans. Kieran Kavanaugh, O.C.D., and Otilio Rodriguez, O.C.D. (Washington, D.C.: ICS Publications, 1991), stanza 1.

24. *The Living Flame of Love*, in *The Collected Works of St. John*, stanza 1, par. 12.

25. Smet, 3, 36.

26. John of St.-Samson's musical abilities were apparently highly developed. He is reported to have been able to play two types of keyboard instruments, four stringed instruments, and three woodwinds. For further details of his life and a study of his poetry see Robert Stefanotti, *The Phoenix of Rennes*. (Peter Lang Publishers, 1994).

27. John of St.-Samson left more than four thousand pages of dictated notes. A critical edition of his collected works has been prepared by Hein Blommestijn, O. Carm., of the Titus Brandsma Institute in Nijmegen.

28. Smet, 3, 57.

Chapter Two

THE FLAMING ARROW

An Early Plea to Return to the Desert

This chapter highlights a unique document in the order's history. Very early in the development of the Carmelite tradition, a general of the order wrote a letter complaining about the order's loss of its contemplative spirit, which, he believed, was being dissipated as Carmelites began to minister in the cities of Europe. In this letter he challenges the Carmelites to remember their original vision. He reminds them of their desert origins.

This chapter and the following one focus on Carmel's analysis of the obstacles which block our spiritual journey. These forces frustrate our deepest desires, and they hinder our relationship with God. The Carmelites consistently agree on the ultimate challenge: *determining who or what will be God in our life*. The challenge or problem may be posed in various ways: In what or whom do we ultimately trust? Where do we look for our affirmation, validation, security? What is our foothold or anchor in life?

The disappointed general believed the order had fashioned idols for itself in the cities. Teresa of Avila and John of the Cross analyzed the problem as one of false selves and false gods. Their contributions will be presented in the next chapter.

Carmel and the Desert

The first Carmelites identified with certain ideals of the desert-dwellers of Egypt and the Middle East. Anthony, who shut himself up in an abandoned fort for many years, and Pachomius who organized large communities of ascetics, went apart from the society of their day to do battle in the desert with demonic forces. They left the temptations of the cities and empires and faced the temptations of the devil in vast wildernesses.

The early Carmelites went into the solitude of the desert to focus their lives exclusively on God. Their mountain was the land of Elijah, whose sojourns in the desert led later generations to identify him as the paradigm of the monk. In solitude, life is met in its starkest terms. One either passes through the desert victorious, or one succumbs. The Carmelite was encouraged to make his cell a desert within the desert, to stay in or near it day and night meditating on the law of the Lord.

Carmel's solitude, in the midst of Crusader and Muslim conflict, forced an encounter within the hermit. Letting go of all external footholds, the hermit opened himself to the war within. The Carmelite entered a realm of both good and bad spirits. The heart of the Carmelite became the battlefield on which the forces of freedom and the forces of slavery fought.

Desert literature understood inner life as a combat with the demons as adversaries. The Rule of Carmel is, in part, desert literature. It warned of the devil on the prowl seeking to ambush souls and devour them. In order to defeat the foe, the Carmelite is urged to put on God's armor: a breastplate of justice, a shield of faith, and a helmet of salvation; he is to take up the sword of the spirit.[1] The Rule reminded the Carmelite of Isaiah's words: Your strength will lie in silence and hope.[2]

A desert carefully tended becomes a garden. In the imagination of Carmelites, Mount Carmel represents not only the solitude in which the hermit wrestles demons, but it also represents the flowering of new, verdant life. The invitation to Carmel offered by the tradition is an invitation to open one's life to the loving activity of God and so to the blossoming of one's life. The garden is a counter-symbol to the desert. Mount Carmel represented solitude and stark battle to the Carmelite, but it was also a place of physical beauty which offered fresh water, thick forest, striking vistas, and the company of wild animals.

The Flaming Arrow

A struggle arose within this young community when it moved to Europe and joined the ranks of the mendicants. Nicholas the Frenchman, Prior General of the order, warned these desert warriors that they would be defeated by the cities of Europe. His letter, remembered in the order as *The Flaming Arrow (Ignea Sagitta)*, urged a retreat back to the slopes of Mount Carmel, if not literally, then wherever and however such an eremitical life can be established.[3] The city was undermining the Carmelite charism of an individual hermit living in a community of hermits. The deeper societal involvement was robbing the hermit of his solitude and causing dissension in his communal life. For the desert-dweller, the city was a place of temptation and danger. The sophistication of the city was eyed warily by those who lived in rusticity.

The Flaming Arrow is the earliest document on record produced from within the order itself. Since the letter is dated 1270, only twenty-three years after the Rule was finalized by Innocent IV, it has been hypothesized, with no evidence however, that Nicholas may have lived on Mount Carmel. His is one of the more vigorous defenses of the eremitical life written in the Middle Ages. If we can reach back over the centuries in empathy, Nicholas becomes a remarkably accessible person.

Nicholas' letter, which is quite a lengthy tract, uses as a framework the situation of a mother (the order) dealing with her stepsons (the innovators in the cities) and her legitimate sons (those who remain faithful to the eremitical ideal). In the letter Nicholas addresses, at different times, the mother and her two sets of sons.

Nicholas grieves at the decadence brought upon the mother by the stepsons. He personally has suffered as general of this community: "...where my own interior life is concerned, when I realize how much time I have lost I find anguish wherever I turn, and no amount of consolation can assuage my grief."[4] But the elaboration of these complaints he reserves for later; for now, his thoughts are on the suffering of the order. Formerly, she was esteemed among all the orders "for the greater sureness of your secret contemplation."[5] But now the order is embroiled in the city and Nicholas has contempt for what he considers deceitful justifications. He disdainfully rehearses them:

> "We have not the least intention of resisting the divine will, but of conforming to it; for our purpose is to edify the people of God, preaching his word, hearing confessions, giving advice, and performing other good works, to our own profit and that of our neighbors. This, rightly and properly is our wholehearted desire. This is the reason–and a very good one–why we left the desert's solitude to come and carry out these works amid the throngs of the cities."[6]

Nicholas then asks the mother for permission to castigate these wayward stepsons who have abandoned the desert life for the city. They think they are better serving themselves and their neighbor when ministering in the cities, but, in fact, both were better served in solitude.

> As long as you persevered in solitude in your contemplations, your prayers and holy exercises, with profit to yourselves, the renown of your holiness, wafted abroad like a perfume, far and wide, over city and town, brought wonderful comfort to all those it reached; and it attracted many, in those days, to the solitude of the desert, edified by its fragrance, and drawn, as though by a cord of tenderness, to repent of their misdeeds.[7]

He argues that such religious should be "different" (we would say counter-cultural), but the Carmelites are no longer different and it is to their shame. When people see that these men "are no different from themselves in their vicious ways, they may sometimes praise them to their faces, but behind their backs they deride them and hold them up to ridicule, for they rightly deem them of little worth."[8]

Nicholas is particularly appalled by Carmelite preaching. It is not actually an attack on the introduction of ministry as mendicants. Even on Mount Carmel there apparently was a limited ministry which included preaching from time to time. Nicholas remembered:

> Sometimes, however, though rarely, they came down from their desert, anxious, so as not to fail in what they regarded as their duty, to be of service to their neighbors and sowed broadcast of the grain, threshed out in preaching, that they had so sweetly reaped in solitude with the sickle of contemplation.[9]

Nicholas complains, however, that the Carmelites in the cities are not properly trained for this ministry, nor do their lives warrant that they be heard. Carmelites had established houses near the theological schools of the day, such as Cambridge (1247), Oxford (1253), Paris (1259) and Bologna (1260), but they did not begin attending such schools until 1271. They were practicing a lay preaching, prevalent in the mendicant groups, which did not require formal study. Nicholas castigated them:

> They prate away before the common folk—without understanding a word of their own rigmarole—as boldfaced as though all theology lay digested in the stomach of their memory, and any tale will serve their turn if it can be given a mystical twist and made to redound to their own glory. Then, when they have done preaching—or rather tale-telling, there they stand, ears all pricked up and itching, to catch the slightest whisper of flattery but not a vestige do they show of the endowments for which, in their appetite for vainglory, they long to be praised.
>
> What is it indeed but a foolish craving for human praise and the vain glory it occasions that moves men like these to preach, devoid as they are of learning and right conduct alike? If they achieve anything at all by their words, they bring it to naught again by their example. The ambitious presumption, the consummate impudence of these unlettered creatures, whose

> moral conduct deserves nothing but contempt, in trying to usurp the office of preaching, is not only an abuse, it is sheer absurdity.[10]

Nicholas has no better opinion of the Carmelites' ability to hear confessions and counsel people. These "illiterates" cannot diagnose one disease from another: "Ignorant alike of theology and law, they are unable to distinguish between one form of leprosy and another, loose what should not be loosed, and bind what should not be bound....It is hard to refrain from laughter...."[11]

Surely there were many Carmelites who were able to preach and counsel competently. Nicholas rejects that opinion; he could not find them. He reminds the reader that as general he has traveled throughout the order and observed Carmelites in many provinces engaged in their ministries. He has sadly concluded: "...how very few there are who have knowledge enough or aptitude for these offices."[12]

The order is rife with "earthly attachments" and "unseemly rovings."[13] Nicholas does not recognize this "new order that has appeared in the cities...."[14] He is not impressed with the mobility of these erstwhile mendicants:

> The main reason for your wanderings is to visit not orphans but young women, not widows in their adversity but silly girls' in dalliance, beguines, nuns, and highborn ladies. Once in their company you gaze into each other's eyes and utter words fit for lovers, the downfall of right conduct and a snare to the heart.[15]

At the very least, Nicholas wanted preaching reserved to those who were actually studying theology. But he also wanted the order to resist a deepening engagement in ministry. Among the reasons for Nicholas' opposition to such ministry was that it called the Carmelite from places of solitude outside the cities to places within the cities. Carmelite houses now were a cluster of rooms in a single building rather than a cluster of huts, caves, or cells arranged in a countryside.

> Was it not for a purpose that he (the Holy Spirit) laid down in our rule that "each one is to have a separate cell"? It does not say "contiguous" but "separate," in order that the heavenly Bridegroom and his Bride, the contemplative soul, might converse the more secretly as they repose therein....But you city dwellers, who have exchanged your separate cells for a common house, what spiritual task do you perform there in full view of one another, what are your holy occupations? When do you ponder God's Law and watch at your prayers?[16]

Nicholas' complaint about the noise and busyness of the Carmelite houses in the city is reminiscent of Teresa of Avila's difficulties with life in the convent of the Incarnation in Avila, although Teresa's nuns did not seem to be as restless as the friars described by Nicholas:

> What use to you in the city are cells that no one enters except at bedtime, so that he might sleep and rest in greater security? As I said you scurry about the lanes and streets of the city at random all day–do you not?–and as soon as you get home, down you sit, cheek by jowl, to exchange rumors and gossip. Why, your whole day's labor is vanity. You reserve your empty cells for sleep alone–do you not?–and spend a third of the night, if not half, in foolish chatter and immoderate tippling. Cells are of no use to those whose thoughts and pastimes are vain. They are for those who make prayer their business.[17]

Nicholas argues that the mitigation in the Rule of 1247 which states that Carmelites may make foundations in solitary places, *or in other suitable and convenient locations given them*, has been misinterpreted. The intent was not to make foundations in cities where the spirit of the Rule would be endangered. He argues that "unsuitable and inconvenient sites should not lead to the introduction of a way of life foreign to our order...."[18]

The uniqueness of the Carmelites does not lie in the three vows, which other religious communities profess. The Lord has placed certain communities in the cities to nourish the people. These communities are learned, are familiar with scripture and live virtuous lives. "Those of a simpler cast, however, those with whom he holds secret colloquy, he marked out to be sent into the desert...."[19] Such are the Carmelites.

Nicholas then stirs the reader's imagination with a portrait of desert life and its blessings. It is not difficult to believe he is reminiscing about Mount Carmel:

> In the desert (*in solitudine*) all the elements conspire to favor us. The heavens, resplendent with the stars and planets in their amazing order, bear witness by their beauty to the mysteries higher still. The birds seem to assume the nature of angels, and tenderly console us with their gentle caroling. The mountains too, as Isaiah prophesied, "drop down sweetness" incomparable upon us, and the friendly hills "flow with milk and honey" such as is never tasted by the foolish lovers of this world. When we sing the praises of our Creator, the mountains about us, our brother conventuals, resound with corresponding hymns of praise to the Lord, echoing back our voices and filling the air with strains of harmony as though accompanying our song upon stringed instruments. The roots in their growth, the grass in its greenness, the leafy boughs and trees–all make merry in their own ways as they echo our praise and the flowers in their loveliness, as they pour out their delicious fragrance, smile their best for the consolation of us solitaries. The sunbeams, though tongueless, speak saving messages to us. The shady bushes rejoice to give us shelter. In short, every creature we see or hear in the desert gives us friendly refreshment and comfort; indeed, for all their silence they tell forth wonders, and move the interior man to give praise to the Creator–so much more wonderful than themselves.

But Nicholas breaks from his reverie:

> ...But in the city, the elements teem with such corruption that you too are contaminated and directly infected.... For melodious birdsong you hear men and women brawling, as well as their animals–mostly dogs and pigs–and an unspeakable din rings in your ears persistently. For green grass and leafy branches you have muddy streets to tramp each day. For the scent of fragrant flowers, your nostrils drink in pestilential draughts of the intolerable stench of depravity.[20]

At the end of his letter, and after having grieved over the terrible state of the order, Nicholas sadly regrets his own inability to change the situation, and he laments what the effort has done to him.

> Ah me! I have so many reasons for sorrow....Who can forbid my grief? For I see that I have made no contribution to the common good in all this time, while I have not been acquiring any merit for myself either.... There can be no recovering a single moment of the time I have lost. I have spent it uselessly, and now I must go back and begin again when I should be drawing to a close.[21]

As disillusioned as he is, Nicholas will not deny his zealous love for the order:

> Is it not my ardent love for you–excessive perhaps–that has kept my soul in such a state of infatuation that I hardly knew who I was, what I was, where I was, or what I should do?
>
> Out of devoted love for you it was that I sailed the seas and journeyed from country to country, that I spent my time and wore out my body; and all my persistent labor for your good, in the face of opposition from your stepsons, has been in vain, for I have brought you no profit. Apart from the merit of my good intentions, then, I count as lost all the heavenly

> treasure I could have been laying up all this time in a solitary cell.[22]

Nicholas concludes by admitting that he never should have been Prior General:

> How could I have presumed, how dared to govern you, I who have never learned to govern myself? How could I have had the audacity to set myself up as a teacher before I had learned to be a pupil, and calmly to pass rash judgment on others before I had learned to examine my own conscience? Alas, Mother! Why did I undertake, in all obedience, to till your field, when it was against the precept of the Law about the ox and the ass–who will not pull together under the same yoke–that I have had to plough?...I have learned always to be cautious in the future.[23]

Nicholas resigned his office as Prior General of the order in 1271.

How *The Flaming Arrow* from Nicholas the Frenchman was received in the Order is not known. Formal theological studies were introduced in 1271. The Carmelites continued their immersion into the Mendicant movement.

The Carmelite Dilemma

The first Carmelites deliberately shed family, possessions, and other forms of security when they went to the solitude of Mount Carmel, there to meet God and the demons, face-to-face. But then events of the first century of the order's existence continued to strip them beyond relinquishings of their own choosing. When they wanted to re-enter European society, now on their own terms, they found difficulty in gaining footholds. The simple life and group anonymity had to be exchanged for newer forms of living which required a deep anchor in the essential values of life on the mountain.

There was no going back to Mount Carmel, which by 1291 had to be completely abandoned. And there was no living in the cities of Europe as though time on the mountain had never happened. The needs were great and the response of the mendicants was a powerful witness to the gospel. Carmelites remained contemplatives, but contemplatives whose prayer opened them to pastoral responses in the Europe of their day.

Whether in the streets of the emerging cities, or in the silence of their cells and oratories, Carmelites returned to their homeland in memory, realizing in a new way the heritage that was theirs. Their mountain was the site of a great contest pitting the faithful Elijah against the prophets of a false god. "How long will you go limping with two different opinions," he cried. "If the Lord is God, follow him; but if Baal, then follow him." (1 Kgs 18:21) It was this Elijah who found himself almost despairing, without strength to go on.

Newer members of the community were taught to respond to inquiries that they were part of a group formed on Mount Carmel and they were in a long line of prayerful people who had lived on the mountain from the time of Elijah and Elisha. The memory haunted them: either follow the Lord God, or follow Baal, but no longer "limp along." In one way or another the struggle against false gods, the realization of their powerlessness, and the surprising, nourishing presence of the true God in their lives would be the constant themes of these Carmelites. They identified with Elijah, and even claimed him as their founder.

Moreover, they increased their devotion to Mary, who had been a model for them from the beginning. They were her brothers, and had prayed in an oratory dedicated to her on Mount Carmel. For them, she modeled a mode of trusting surrender to God's mercy and will. The lives of both Elijah and Mary spoke of an inner structure which was compatible with the desert into which the earlier Carmelites had withdrawn. They spoke of the essence of the desert existence, the true desert, which no longer relies on a specific place and geography.

Nicholas the Frenchman in *The Flaming Arrow* anticipated the complaints of later Carmelite reformers. Long before the sixteenth- and seventeenth-century renewals of Carmel, Nicholas was identifying problems which would be perennial in Carmel. The centered, focused, harmonious life described in the Rule had been abandoned, in his estimation, when the Carmelites left places of solitude to live in the hearts of the cities. There they joined the people in worship of the golden calf while Moses was with God on the mountain.

The quiet hermits had become garrulous rovers! Their preoccupations had brought discord and division to community life. When were they ever alone, he asked, taking time to be with God? Anticipating the critiques of later reformers, including Teresa of Avila and John of the Cross, Nicholas accused Carmelites of idolatry. He condemned their attachments which turned them from freedom to slavery.

NOTES

1. *Albert's Way*, ed. Michael Mulhall, O. Carm. (Rome: Institutum Carmelitanum, 1989), 13–15. See also the Appendix of this present work.
2. Ibid., 17.
3. Nicholas, Prior General of the Carmelite Order, *The Flaming Arrow*, trans. Bede Edwards, in *The Sword* (June, 1979), 3–52.
4. Ibid., 19.
5. Ibid., 18.
6. Ibid., 21.
7. Ibid., 22.
8. Ibid., 22, 23.
9. Ibid., 28.
10. Ibid., 23.
11. Ibid.
12. Ibid., 24.
13. Ibid.
14. Ibid., 25.
15. Ibid.
16. Ibid., 31.
17. Ibid., 32.
18. Ibid., 29.
19. Ibid., 30.
20. Ibid., 36, 37.
21. Ibid., 41.
22. Ibid., 42.
23. Ibid.

Chapter Three

FALSE SELVES AND FALSE GODS

According to Teresa of Avila and John of the Cross

Nicholas the Frenchman, in his letter of lament, mocked the illusions of his beloved Carmelites. What they understood to be necessary adaptations of lifestyle and ministry, he believed to be debilitating attachments. What they offered as evidence of good works and concern for the edification of the people, he dismissed as the products of enslaved hearts which no longer were free to hear God's call. They were following idols created by their own hands. Perhaps Nicholas' critique was partially the result of a dyspeptic disposition, but his observations and analyses contain perennial concerns. He knew the human heart.

Teresa of Avila and John of the Cross, writing primarily for the men and women of the order, made observations which echo and amplify the concerns of Nicholas.

Teresa of Avila and Self-knowledge

The problem in life, said Teresa of Avila, is that we do not know ourselves.[1] We have a certain level of understanding, but, essentially, we do not grasp our reality. We wander outside the castle of our lives, preoccupied with many things, in each of which we search for something more. Teresa said that for eighteen years in the convent she was torn between numerous preoccupations and the call to a deeper living. She wrote: "...for more than eighteen of the twenty-eight years since I began prayer, I suffered this battle and conflict between friendship with God and friendship with the world."[2] She named some of the things which preoccupied her: family, friends, business affairs, possessions. Each was potentially good in itself, but each shouting so loudly for attention that any quieter, steadier call had little chance to be heard. Her heart was scattered in these many centers of her life and she was drawn outside herself.

True self-knowledge is elusive because we ask others who we are; we look to those around us for the identity and affirmation we desperately seek. Teresa gradually realized that she had been seeking self-affirmation in both the society from which she came, and from the religious life she had entered. In both cases she had been looking at herself through others' eyes.

Teresa was particularly vulnerable to society's constrictions. She was a woman, writing in the vernacular, about experiences of God. Any one of those realities was sufficient for suspicion on the part of the learned authorities of the day. It is startling to realize that religious women were not encouraged to go beyond vocal prayer. They were not to reflect within themselves upon the words they were speaking. As part of her reform, Teresa argued for mental prayer. She encouraged her sisters to think inwardly about the realities they were expressing when they said the "Our Father" and "Hail Mary."

Teresa was captivated by the image of the original Carmelites as solitaries in community. She wrote that when she and her sisters could finally enter their new foundations and close the door they breathed a sigh of relief. What seems to us, perhaps, to be a restrictive setting, was a place of freedom for the women of Teresa's reform. Society's norms and judgments were, to a great extent, suspended within the walls of her foundations.

Teresa had another, potentially debilitating, concern which involved social realities in the Spain of her day. Her father was Jewish, and to have Jewish blood was to be vulnerable in sixteenth-century Spain.[3] Teresa's grandfather, a Jewish convert to Christianity, had confessed to the Inquisition in Toledo that he had relapsed, that he had been practicing Judaism in secret. He and his sons, including Teresa's father, were made to join public processions on seven first Fridays in order to atone and be reconciled.

The family moved to Avila. There, apparently, they were able to buy a "certificate of nobility," opening the way to public respect and possible acquisition of wealth. They could display a coat of arms and use the titles Don and Doña. Many in Spain had bought their way into nobility but were resented by the Old Christians who had *limpieza de sangre*, or "purity of blood." The Catholic monarchs enlisted the New Christians in a struggle against the Old Christians for control of Spain.

Over the centuries old families had married into households of "impure" blood. As tensions increased in Spain these families, too, became vulnerable to accusations. The Inquisition, it is thought, was originally begun to monitor the converts to Christianity. If a family were denounced to the Inquisition it could mean disgrace and financial ruin. Teresa's family was in just such a precarious state.

Teresa, the New Christian, saw the possibility in religious life of an "alternative society," just as the early church had been. Studies have shown that some of the first members of her new community of St. Joseph's in Avila shared her background. It suggests she strongly attracted other New Christians and many of her patrons and benefactors also shared her social origins.

(Teresa's foundations attracted the urban middle-class, where you would expect to find New Christians. Her communities also had their share of the needy, as well as the aristocratic. But, apparently, a woman considering entering one of Teresa's communities would normally come from a family of at least moderate means.

Originally, Teresa eliminated dowries for her candidates. Later, she thought it unsuitable if someone brought no dowry, and we read of her commenting favorably upon the suitability of a candidate, in part, based on her potential dowry. While Teresa grew to appreciate the income from dowries, she says she never refused a worthy candidate who had no dowry. Teresa was flexible on the amount of the dowry, but five years after her death the new Order began requiring a fixed dowry once more.

Because of the expectation of a dowry, and because Teresa insisted that candidates be literate, in order to read the Divine Office, the mass of countryfolk were probably excluded from her communities.

By 1581, when her work had just about been completed, records show that most of the sisters in the reformed convents were from urban areas, with the small group of lay sisters coming mainly from rural areas.[4]

The Carmelite Order which Teresa was reforming ["of the cloth," she called them], observed *limpieza de sangre* beginning in 1566, just when Teresa was starting her reform. She, however, regularly admitted New Christians throughout her life. Fifteen years after her death, in 1597, the Discalced Carmelites, now a separate Order, also instituted statutes of purity, forbidding entrance into the community of any person with Jewish or Moorish blood going back four generations. Teresa would not have been accepted into her own Order.

Among her benefactors, too, were New Christians. In founding a house in Toledo Teresa had the support of Alonso Alvarez, a *converso*, or as Teresa wrote, a man whose family was "not from the nobility." Many of the townsfolk complained. She said she did not pay much attention to the criticism because, "I have always esteemed virtue more than lineage."[5]She did have to work out a compromise allowing a wealthy noble family to endow the chapel and Alvarez to help buy the house, "one of the nicest in Toledo," Teresa noted with satisfaction. She wrote, "Our Lord desired to give me light in this matter, and so at one time He told me that lineage and social status mattered not at all in the judgment of God."[6])

Life inside Teresa's new communities did not, however, guarantee the self-knowledge she believed was critical for a Christian. Not only were her sisters not to claim any worth based on their family background, but they were not to substitute another form of hierarchy and privilege based on religious living. Teresa insisted that the goal for her sisters was to want what God wants. The whole purpose of prayer is conformity with God's will. Their ultimate goal is not to be contemplatives, or to have a spiritual life, or to have special experiences in prayer, but to strive to find God's will. With that seeking comes one's true identity and in that relationship one experiences affirmation. Any other foothold in life will not offer true support. Even the very security of a well-ordered life may become an obstacle to deeper penetration of the rooms of the castle.[7]

The self-knowledge Teresa eventually gained consisted of two fundamental truths. The first truth was a realization of her essential poverty. She came to know her inattentiveness to God, her fragmentation and dissipation. She acknowledged her sinfulness. And, on her own, she was absolutely powerless to control her life. Left to her own insight, energy, and vision she was unable to pull her fragmented life together. The harder she tried, she confessed, the more she was stuck. Nor was there anything offered her by society which could validate her life. She realized the essential poverty of her life.

But Teresa counseled that it would be a great mistake to focus solely on our unfaithful and sinful condition. Such an emphasis could lead to a humility in which one is overwhelmed by shortcomings and therefore paralyzed in life. "If we are always fixed on our earthly misery, the stream will never flow free from the mud of fears, faintheartedness, and cowardice."[8] Such a humility undermines a person and defeats any attempts to engage life. This kind of humility, Teresa taught, was one of the most serious temptations of the devil.

The second, and more important, truth about her life was that this poor woman was immensely rich. At the core of her life was a reality which sustained her life, empowered her, and was her truest identity. She knew about God in her mind; she had to learn to trust that God in her experience. She became convinced that we live life buoyed on a sea of mercies. We cannot claim the credit; we can only live with gratitude. Once she knew who she was, fear fell away, and she lived with focused energy.

Her advice was to focus on Jesus, and in the light of that love to know ourselves as we really are. When the primary gaze is on God, then one's poverty can be acknowledged; but it does not become the final word about our existence. The final word is seen in God who continues to love us to health and calls us into union.

This humility makes one buoyant and confident. The world is vigorously engaged, not because we are our own source of strength, but because God is faithful and gives us vision and strength. "So I say, daughters, that we should set our eyes on Christ, our Good, and on His saints. There we shall learn true humility,...and self-knowledge will not make one base and cowardly."[9]

John of the Cross and the Enslaved Heart

John of the Cross identified our basic problem as an "enslaved heart." We continually give our hearts away in adoration at the altar of false gods. Our fundamental desire, he believed, was for the Mystery at the center of our souls, the God of our belief. The only place we are able to meet this God is in the world within and around us. John observed:

Pouring out a thousand graces
He passed these groves in haste
And having looked at them,
With his image alone
clothed them in beauty.[10]

God's creatures introduce us to God. However, in John's analysis, whoever or whatever introduces us to God may soon take God's place. The heart easily mistakes the traces of God for God. That which we can see, touch, taste, feel, hear has the power to transfix us, and the heart, tired of its continual seeking, begins to settle down with lesser gods. We let our lives be slowly centered around this trace of God and ask of it to be ultimate, to be the answer to our deepest desire. John calls this type of relationship an attachment. In an attachment the heart gives itself away in slavery to an idol, asking some part of God's creation to be uncreated.

John's analysis is that whenever we give our hearts away in an attachment, we not only become like that which we love, but we become possessed by our loves, "because love not only equates, but even subjects the lover to the loved creature."[11] The satiation is so distorted that John describes it as slavery. The heart is no longer free to grow in God's love. Hc writes: "...freedom has nothing to do with slavery. And freedom cannot abide in a heart dominated by desires, in a slave's heart. It abides in a liberated heart, in a child's heart."[12]

John observes how our desires are never satisfied and so they weary and tire us: "Just as a lover is wearied and depressed when on a longed for day his opportunity is frustrated...."[13] We become sluggish in the things of God and cold in our charity toward our neighbors. Virtue becomes a burden. The suffering caused by our appetites is compared to lying on nails, or being held prisoner, chained to our appetites. And they do not have to be great attachments. Small ones can be corrosive as well, such as,

> the common habit of being very talkative; a small attachment one never really desires to conquer, for example, to a person, to clothing, to a book or a cell, or to the way food is prepared, and to other trifling conversations and little satisfactions in tasting, knowing, and hearing things, and so on.[14]

It does not take much for one's freedom of spirit to be severely impaired: "It makes little difference whether a bird is tied by a thin thread or by a cord."[15]

The enslaved heart results in two deaths: whoever or whatever we are asking to be our God cannot bear the expectation. We begin to smother our loves by asking them to be more than they can be. Not only do our loves begin to die under the pressures, but we ourselves begin to die. We cannot grow past our god; a lesser god means a lesser self. Nothing (*nada*) is sufficient food for our hungers, except the God who is No-thing.

A Carmelite Perspective

Does the analysis of the Carmelites hold true today? Are we still struggling with demonic forces, wayward desires, enslaved hearts? As anachronistic as the language sometimes is, people who hear this tradition recognize their own struggles in it. The heart that is enslaved with a relationship, or by possessions, or has been caught in addictions recognizes a description of its plight in John of the Cross.

Whatever preoccupies or absorbs us to the neglect of a true center in our lives becomes a false god. Locked into possessions, relationships, projects, societal expectations, identities in such a way that we are locked out of our selves and the core of that self, we are kept on the periphery of our lives. It is a life of unreality. We are unable to see things, and live them, as they truly are.

We, in our tight grasp, turn others and things into whatever we need them to be. The child is turned into an extension of ourselves. The community is used to feed us. The ministry or project is distorted because it serves our unacknowledged needs. Our prayers become bargaining.

The heart cannot stop yearning for fulfillment, hungering for nourishment. Unable to trust in an Unknown Presence, the heart fixes on what is at hand, often compulsively. Attachments, ways of asking God's creation to be God, lead to addictions, behaviors which feed on the insubstantial.

And Teresa's complaint that we do not truly know ourselves (false self), becomes more and more convincing to one who has been forced to make an inner journey for one reason or another. On that journey, either in analysis with a therapist, or simply through greater listening to one's life, the unknown parts of the self begin to emerge. Initially, the shadow side of the self almost defeats the effort to grow. It is too painful to meet and acknowledge. With the deeper awareness of the inauthentic ways we have been living, comes also a greater sense of our sinfulness. Our poverty may be extreme and we can only acknowledge it, in silence and in hope.

The concrete life issues that often bring us to our knees in an admission of powerlessness are infinitely varied. But the human spirit is often compelled to lay down its arms and admit to no further strength or vision, like Elijah in the desert. All a person can do is wait. And that is when the possibility of reconstructing life, but on a different basis, becomes a reality. What on the surface seems to be an adult crisis, at depth may be a challenge to one's faith. In what or whom can I place my trust as I proceed in life? On what foundation can I count as I begin to rebuild? Where is my true strength?

Teresa of Avila and John of the Cross provided extended analyses of problems which earlier generations would have recognized. False selves and false gods are a perennial problem. The first Carmelites wrestled with them as hermits; they encountered them again in Europe. They continually reminded themselves of their primary activity: a prayerful encounter with God whose love undermines all false claims and restores health to the soul.

Carmelites were challenged to carry within them the very conditions they had experienced around them on Mount Carmel. The silence of the wadi now had to be an inner stillness. The silence had to be so interiorized that whether preaching in the streets or reflecting in their cells, at the core of their activity was a quiet listening. The solitude of the wadi now had to be translated into an inner desert which accompanied the Carmelite in any situation. In the first two centuries of the order's existence these contemplative themes found ever newer expression as the tradition deepened.

NOTES

1. Teresa of Avila, *The Interior Castle,* in *The Collected Works of St. Teresa of Avila*, 2, trans. Kieran Kavanaugh, O.C.D., and Otilio Rodriguez, O.C.D. (Washington, D.C.: ICS Publications, 1980), The First Dwelling Places, chap. 1, no. 2.

2. *The Book of Her Life*, in *The Collected Works*, 1, chap. 8, no. 3.

3. In 1492, not too long before Teresa's birth in 1515, Ferdinand and Isabella captured the last Moorish stronghold of Granada, uniting Spain after an eight hundred-year effort to reconquer it from the Moors.

The Jewish population lived principally among the Moors. As Spain was slowly united through the fourteenth and fifteenth centuries, with the church being the most important unifying force, more and more pressure was put on the Jews to convert. In the same year Ferdinand and Isabella captured Granada all unconverted Jews were expelled from Spain.

The converted Jews were called *conversos*, or New Christians. Decrees were passed barring *conversos* from most major religious orders, including the Carmelites, from civic offices, and from senior colleges at the Universities. By the time Teresa was beginning her reforms *limpieza de sangre* (purity of blood) was a critical concern in practically all public life. Cf. Rowan Williams, *Teresa of Avila* (Harrisburg, PA: Morehouse Publishing, 1991).

4. Cf. Teofanes Egido, "The Economic Concerns of Madre Teresa," in *Carmelite Studies*, IV, ed. John Sullivan, O.C.D. (Washington, D.C.: ICS Publications, 1987).

5. Teresa of Avila, *The Foundations,* in *The Collected Works,* 3, chap. 15, no. 15.

6. Ibid., no. 16.

7. "The great danger is in supposing that our regular and controlled lives give us some sort of claim upon God, so that we become bitterly resentful if God is apparently not at home to us in the way we should like." Williams, *Teresa of Avila*, 118.

8. Teresa of Avila, *Interior Castle,* in *The Collected Works*, 2, The First Dwelling Places, chap. 2, no. 10.

9. Ibid., no. 11.

10. John of the Cross, "Spiritual Canticle," in *The Collected Works of St. John of the Cross*, trans. Kieran Kavanaugh, O.C.D., and Otilio Rodriguez, O.C.D. (Washington, D.C.: ICS Publications, 1991), stanza 5.

11. John of the Cross, *The Ascent of Mount Carmel,* in *The Collected Works,* Book 1, chap. 4, no. 3.

12. Ibid., no. 6.

13. Ibid., chap 6, no. 6.

14. Ibid., chap. 11, no 4.

15. Ibid.

Chapter Four

THE INSTITUTION OF THE FIRST MONKS

Carmel's Foundational Story

The earliest Carmelites attacked the problem of egoism, disordered desires, and enslaved hearts through a disciplined life which combined elements of prayer, fasting, silence, solitude, and work. These were the time-honored weapons of desert dwellers. They put on the armor of faith. Each man was told to stay in or near his cell "pondering on the Lord's law day and night, and keeping watch at his prayers...." He was to abstain from meat, fasting every day from the Feast of The Exaltation of the Holy Cross until Easter (i.e., most of the year). These men owned everything in common, each living on what was given him by the prior, whom he was to reverence.

With these weapons the Carmelite entered the interior desert, willing to face whatever dangerous powers lived there. They opened themselves to the currents within their souls and the full force of their own untamed thoughts and desires. The structures of their life undermined their willfulness. Steeping themselves in scripture, they lived trustingly in the presence of God.[1]

In the beginning these men lived quite solitary lives on Mount Carmel, but always with the assumption that they were a community of men in the Christian body. Consequently, eucharist together, daily if possible, was a value. And each week they met to correct and encourage one another.

As time went on, and especially in the new conditions in

Europe, the community dimension was strengthened. They began to pray the psalms together at stipulated times each day, and they began to come together at mealtimes as well. The hermits of Mount Carmel rather quickly became friars in Europe.

The Carmelite Order never disowned its original contemplative inspiration. No matter how neglectful of its calling, no matter how preoccupied with new forms of ministry, Carmelites clung to their foundation in contemplative prayer, which for the early Carmelites took the form of ruminating on scripture, listening for God's approach in their lives. Whenever they rose up to claim their identity or to renew their lives, they returned in spirit to the wadi on Mount Carmel and held up as a privileged activity for all Carmelites the silent encounter with God deep within the human soul.

The call to "watch in prayer" was a constant exhortation. Even though the order had become a mendicant community heavily involved in service of God's people, it was not evident in the order's documents. Carmelites wrote as though they were still living an eremitical life on Mount Carmel, and did not seem to notice any discrepancy with their actual lives. Apparently the contemplative activity, which was often associated with being in their cells, being quiet, being alone, was actually an activity which accompanied, but was different from, whatever else they were doing. Contemplation was another level of human activity, an attentiveness, which may or may not manifest itself in obvious "contemplative" lifestyles, structures, or activities. They would not have understood a dichotomy between contemplation and their pastoral activity.

The Carmelite Rule, which received its final formulation in 1247, and is still the Rule today, gives little hint that Carmelites are doing any more than praying in their cells, working in silence, and occasionally coming together for prayer and meals. Yet, Carmelites have served the church for eight hundred years in innumerable pastoral activities, and have expressed no discomfort with the Rule. When reform was required, as it often was, it was not the ministries of the Carmelites which were criticized. It was their base in contemplative prayer that was questioned (along with the observance of the common life and poverty). What they actually were doing day to day in the church and for the church was never the point. All reforms called Carmelites back to the contemplative ideal which finds its expression in the Rule.

The earliest documents generally spoke about prayer, but very little about ministry. The disappointed general, Nicholas the Frenchmen, in his 1270 letter to the order, *The Flaming Arrow*, argued for a more literal interpretation of the Rule. He urged the men to stop roaming the streets and to get back into their cells. He said they should abandon the cities and return to the rural settings. Only those conditions would allow the heavenly Bridegroom and his Bride to "converse the more secretly as they repose therein...." in contemplative prayer.[2]

But Nicholas' exhortations were met with silence. Almost all Carmelite houses founded in the first century of the order's existence, before and after Nicholas' letter, were located in urban settings. Being in the cities and spending time ministering to the people was never really the problem for most Carmelites. Perhaps they instinctively knew that a contemplative spirit, a "listening heart," was possible in any condition.

The *Rubrica Prima* from the Constitutions of 1281, which probably originated in the 1240s, told Carmelites to identify themselves as men who came from a long line of contemplatives on Mount Carmel going back to the prophets Elijah and Elisha. It did not tell Carmelites to take their stand as mendicants, which they certainly were by then. The General Chapter of 1287 wrote that "we have left the world to be able to serve our Creator effectively in the castle of contemplation."[3]

The Carmelite story began to take on its distinctive contours over the first two centuries of the order's existence. The order's identity very quickly coalesced around contemplative prayer and the figures of Elijah and Mary.

The Institution of the First Monks

At the end of the fourteenth century a Carmelite provincial from Catalonia, Philip Ribot (d. 1391), told the story of Carmel in a new, more coherent way. Ribot pulled together various traditions in the order, particularly the Elijan and Marian traditions and provided a foundational myth which coalesced a variety of themes and values.

Ribot supposedly collected four separate works and arranged them in ten books.[4] The first seven books constitute the most important work, *Liber de institutione primorum monachorum*, or *The Institution of the First Monks*.[5] It probably circulated in the order in the 1390s. Today it is considered the second most important document in the order, after the Rule, for the development of Carmelite spirituality. The medieval imagination is evident as a "history" of Carmel is woven from diverse scriptural texts.

The Institution of the First Monks has two parts: the first part presents the ascetical and mystical ideal of Carmel; the second part constructs an imaginative history of the Carmelite Order from the time of Elijah down to New Testament times. The *Institution* purports to have been written in Greek in 412. It takes the form of a letter from the Bishop of Jerusalem, John XLIV, who supposedly had been a hermit on Mount Carmel, to a young Carmelite, Caprasius. It begins, "With good reason, Caprasius, you inquire about the beginning of the Order....we shall presently begin to speak of the supreme Founder of the Order...."[6] The "Founder" is none other than the prophet Elijah!

Noting that Elijah was the first of all monks, the origin of monastic life, the bishop refers to the key scriptural text which organizes this first part of the *Institution*: "And the word of the Lord came to him [Elijah], '*Depart from here and turn eastward and hide yourself by the brook Cherith, that is east of the Jordan. You shall drink from the brook, and I have commanded the ravens to feed you there*' (1 Kgs 17:2–4)."[7]

This text is then interpreted to contain four steps which will lead the hermit to the contemplative experience of God.

1. *Depart from here* refers to a detachment from "the perishable things of the world, relinquishing in spirit and in reality for my sake, all earthly possessions and powers...."[8]

2. *Turn eastward* means a renunciation of sin, taking up the cross, a turn "against the original cupidity of your flesh."[9]

3. *Hide yourself by the brook Cherith* is a command to "live in the hidden solitude of silence."[10]

4. *East of the Jordan* is the situation of one who lives in charity (in Cherith); love of God and neighbor set the monk east of the Jordan, "that is, against the descent of sins..."[11]

The goal of this graced ascetical effort is to be a contemplative, to experience the presence of God.

> Therefore, when you come to the goal of the prophetic and eremitical, monastic life and thus are hidden "in Cherith," that is in charity, then there "you shall drink from the brook," because in this so perfect union of yourself with me, I shall give you and your companions to drink from that brook of which the prophet, speaking to me, says: "you give them drink from the river of your delights" (Ps 36:9).[12]

The hermit/Carmelite will not be able to live in a continuous contemplative state enjoying God's presence. Consequently, *I have commanded the ravens to feed you there.* The ravens are the prophets who are models for the monk, because they remember their sins and acknowledge their frailty.

> I have commanded the prophets, your holy predecessors, that they should feed you by the doctrine of examples of humble contrition, by which they humbly recognized in themselves the blackness of sin and avoided the brightness of carnal life.[13]

A "History" of the Carmelites

Books Two to Five of *The Institution of the First Monks* tell an imaginative "history" of the Carmelites, beginning with Elijah as the founder and model of religious life. He is joined in the wadi Cherith by others who are fleeing the persecution of Jezebel.[14] Elijah teaches them to be prophets, "that is, to sing canticles, hymns and psalms, accompanied with musical instruments, for the glory of God."[15]

Since they began their common life in the wadi Cherith, why were Carmelites not called "Cherithites"? Because the wadi lacked water and was not habitable.[16] Elijah, hunted by Queen Jezebel, had to live as a wandering fugitive, "now in the desert at the torrent of Cherith, now in the widow's house at Sarepta, again in the desert of Bersabea or in a cave on Mount Horeb."[17] His followers, too, had to wander from place to place. "Therefore, since they could not live in peace at Cherith or anywhere else, they cannot be called Cherithites from Cherith."[18]

On Horeb, Elijah learns that the wind, the earthquake, and the fire are forms of destruction for those who were not faithful to God. But the "gentle air" promises a restoration:

> The whistling of a gentle air symbolized Elijah, whom the Lord showed in the vision that he would traverse the kingdom of Israel like the whistling of a gentle air calling his disciples and the other servants of God to the refreshment of peace after the cessation of their persecutions.[19]

When he returned from Horeb, Elijah gathered his disciples on Mount Carmel. He chose that place because Carmel was the most suitable of all places for living the prophetic, monastic life.

> The mountain does indeed afford silence and quiet to a hermit because of its solitude; shelter in its caves; peace in its woodlands; healthful air from its elevation; abundant food from its herbs and fruits; and delicious water from its springs.[20]

They built a house for prayer, called the Semnion, and gathered in it three times a day, playing their musical instruments, singing hymns, psalms, and canticles, and listening to readings from scripture.

Elijah was the first monk, the perfect model of the religious. His first disciple was Jonah, the widow's son whom he raised from the dead. He is the one whom Elijah would send to look for the cloud on Mount Carmel. So many others joined him that they lived in places in the desert and in the cities, places such as Gilgal, Bethel and Jericho.

Elijah lived sixteen years on Mount Carmel, and so the mountain is holy. He worked miracles there, such as the defeat of the prophets of Baal; he called Israel back to faithfulness to God. Life on Mount Carmel was a life of justice and peace. "As the Prophet Isaias, in the person of the Lord, foretold about them and their dwelling place: 'Judgment shall dwell in the wilderness, and justice shall sit in Carmel, and the work of justice shall be peace, and the service of justice, quietness, and security forever. And my people shall sit in the beauty of peace, and in the tabernacles of confidence, and in wealthy rest' (Is 32:16–18)."[21]

Although they stayed mainly on Mount Carmel and in other desert locations, the Carmelites would occasionally visit towns to work miracles, to call people back to God, and to draw new members to the order. After a period of probation in the cities, new members welcomed living in the solitude of the desert.

With the order firmly established, Elijah, in a chariot of fiery horses, was taken up to heaven in a whirlwind of fire. Elijah, and Enoch, are to return to prepare the day of the Lord in the time of the Antichrist. Elisha, the greatest of his disciples, had received the spirit of Elijah; he was given Elijah's habit to symbolize that spirit. It was the duty of Elisha, now, to rule and teach the community. Elisha visited the various communities consoling them and showing them signs and wonders. "All the monks received him in Elijah's place as their chief father and master."[22] He governed the communities wisely, teaching them to trust in God.

Because of their faithfulness and their peaceful life on Mount Carmel, God spared the Carmelites from being taken captive by the Babylonians. They lived in hope of the Messiah.

When John the Baptist came in the spirit of Elijah, Carmelites were living near the Jordan. They heard him preach and they were baptized. In the time of Christ, the Carmelites had a house in Jerusalem, near the upper room. Shortly after the ascension they were gathered in Jerusalem to celebrate Jewish feasts. On the day of Pentecost they heard Peter preach and they realized John had prepared them for this moment, and so they were baptized in Christ.

Some Carmelites hesitated and were praying in the temple the next day. They witnessed Peter healing a crippled man, and they heard him preach about the resurrection of Jesus. "They believed completely in Jesus–five thousand–who, after being baptized by the Apostles, received the Holy Ghost in the form of visible fire."[23]

And so the Carmelites became Christians. They were faithful to the teaching of the apostles, and to the celebration of the breaking of the bread. They prayed daily in the temple. They studied scripture, and through allegorical interpretation, sought spiritual and invisible meanings.

> Finally, many of them pouring out to others the doctrines they had drawn from the Apostles, preached the faith of Christ in Phoenicia and Palestine, explaining the dogmas of faith and, by the practices of the monastic life, demonstrating the marvelous way of life taught by the Church of Christ.[24]

Mary in the Tradition

The Marian tradition is united with the Elijan tradition in Book Six of the *Institution*.[25] When Elijah sends his servant to look out to sea, the servant reports seeing a small cloud. To the prostrate Elijah, God revealed four mysteries in this vision of the little cloud: 1) the future birth of a girl born without sin; 2) the time of her birth; 3) that she would be the first woman to take the vow of virginity (after Elijah who was the first man to vow virginity); 4) that the Son of God would be born of this virgin.

The Carmelites, now Christians, understood that these mysteries were fulfilled in Mary.[26] "...Before the Mother of God passed from this life, she was seen frequently by the members of our institute in Nazareth, Jerusalem, and elsewhere."[27] The Carmelites devoted themselves to Mary and chose her as their Patroness. In A.D. 83, they replaced the ancient Semnion with a chapel in Mary's honor, near the font of Elijah where the little cloud had been seen. Mary was their sister, and they were known as the Brothers of the Blessed Virgin of Mount Carmel.

(The Marian tradition, found in the *Institution,* has early traces in the Order's history, but not in some of the places where one would expect to find it. Mary is not mentioned in the Carmelite Rule. Nor is she mentioned in the *Rubrica Prima* of the 1281 Constitutions. *The Flaming Arrow* has only a passing reference to her.

But the Rule does mandate that an oratory be established in the middle of the cells, and early pilgrim reports testify to a church in the wadi dedicated to Our Lady. As early as 1252 papal documents contain the title "Brothers of Our Lady of Mount Carmel.[28] Peter of Millau, prior general in 1282 wrote to King Edward I of England asking for protection and promising prayer to "the most glorious Virgin...to whose praise and glory the Order itself was specially instituted in parts beyond the sea."[29] The Constitutions of 1294 required that the name of Mary be given in response to inquiries about the Order or its name.[30] These same Constitutions, for the first time, refer to Mary as patroness of the Order.

By the time of the 1324 Constitutions the *Rubrica Prima* spoke of both Elijan and Marian origins adding: "After the Incarnation their successors built a church there [on Mount Carmel] in honor of the Blessed Virgin Mary, and chose her title; therefore from that time they were by apostolic privilege called the Brothers of Blessed Virgin Mary of Mount Carmel."[31]

Jean de Cheminot in 1337 related Elijah and Mary through their vows of virginity. He apparently was the first to identify Elijah and Elisha as founders of the Carmelites.

The English Carmelite, John Baconthorpe [d. 1348], also linked the Elijan and Marian traditions in his works. He perhaps was the first to understand the small cloud seen by Elijah as a symbol of Mary.

Baconthorpe's commentary on the Rule is a creative and quaint comparison of Mary's life with elements in the Rule, e.g. the Rule requires each one to have a separate cell; the angel Gabriel found Mary contemplating in her own room. An oratory is to be built in the middle of the cells; Mary was brought by her parents to the temple. The Carmelite is to remain in or near his cell meditating; Mary prayed many hours each day. The Rule requires silence; Mary speaks no more than four times in the Gospels. Carmelites may keep asses and mules; Mary rode an ass not a horse. The prior is to serve the others; Mary stayed with Elizabeth for three months. And so forth.[32])

Ribot; in the *Institution*, is credited with the first true synthesis of the Elijan and Marian traditions in the Order. Later, the Carmelite humanist Arnold Bostius (d.1499) produced his own, mature synthesis of the order's traditions. Bostius presented Elijah and Mary as co-founders of Carmel, with Mary having priority. Her example and future destiny inspired Elijah to found the order.

The Carmelite habit is the theme of the final Book Seven of the *Institution*. In this book the habit is a sign of poverty, humility, separation from the world, dedication to God, and of a common fraternity. The scapular is understood as the yoke of obedience.

(For approximately 150 years the scapular was identified not with Mary but with obedience, a Christological theme. The first reference to it is in the Constitutions of 1281: "the Brothers are to sleep in their tunic and scapular under pain of severe penalty."[33] No mention is made of a scapular vision to St. Simon Stock in thirteenth-century documents.

A late-fourteenth-century account tells of Mary appearing to Simon Stock, who, perhaps, was elected prior general in 1254 at the general chapter of London. She held the scapular in her hand and said that the one who dies in it will be saved.[34] It is not possible to verify the historicity of this event which only surfaces in accounts almost 150 years after the purported event. A contemporary approach to this devotion understands the scapular as an expression of devotion to Mary, a sign of her protection and care, and a willingness to imitate her prayerful submission to God's salvific plan.)

The Elijan-Marian synthesis in the *Institution* presents a richly textured spirituality for the order. The order has two models, both witnessing to a contemplative attentiveness and availability to God. In them we see the Carmelite ideal as expressed in the words of the *Institution*:

> The goal of this life is twofold. One part we acquire, with the help of divine grace, through our efforts and virtuous works. This is to offer God a holy heart, free from all stain of actual sin. We do this when we are perfect and in Cherith, that is hidden in that charity of which the Wise man says: "Charity covers all offences"(Prv 10:12). God desired Elijah to advance thus far, when He said to him: "Hide yourself by the brook Cherith."
>
> The other part of the goal of this life is granted us as the free gift of God: namely, to taste somewhat in the heart and to experience in the soul, not only after death but even in this mortal life, the intensity of the divine presence and the sweetness of the glory of heaven. This is to drink of the torrent of the love of God. God promised it to Elijah in the words: "You shall drink from the brook."[35]

Perhaps an image capturing the core theme of the *Institution* is that of Elijah sitting at the mouth of his cave at the wadi Cherith being fed by a raven. Elijah living in God's presence models the eremitical spirit for Carmelites.

The ascetical ideal, offering to God a pure and holy heart, opens to the mystical ideal, experiencing in mind and heart the presence of God which is pure gift.

NOTES

1. The Rule of Carmel has at least eight places where the hermit is encouraged to read, listen to, reflect on, or pray scripture. A traditional form of prayer was a faithful rumination on the scripture called *lectio divina*. The expression comes from Origen and refers to a prayerful reading of scripture with attentiveness and openness to God speaking through the Word.

In the twelfth century this approach was systematized into four steps by Guido, a Carthusian monk: "On a certain day, during manual work, when I was thinking about the activity of the human spirit, suddenly in my mind I could see the ladder of the four spiritual steps, *lectio, meditatio, oratio,* and *contemplatio*."

The faith-filled reading of *scripture (lectio)* leads to thoughtful reflection on what has been read *(meditatio)*, which results in ardent prayer to God *(oratio)*, and this prayer ends in silent commune with and enjoyment of God whose presence has been revealed through scripture *(contemplatio)*. Cf. Carlos Mesters, O. Carm., "The Carmelite Rule and the Reading of the Bible: Reflections on Lectio Divina," in *Carmelite Charism* (Melbourne: Carmelite Communications, 1991), 11–30.

2. Nicholas, Prior General of the Carmelite Order, *The Flaming Arrow*, trans. Bede Edwards, O.C.D., in *The Sword* (June, 1979), 31.

3. Joachim Smet, O. Carm., *The Carmelites*, 1 (Darien, IL.: Carmelite Spiritual Center, 1988), 19.

4. His collection is titled *Decem libri de institutione et peculiaribus gestis religiosorum carmelitarum. (Ten Books concerning the Institution and Deeds of the Carmelites)*. The suspicion of scholars is that Ribot is the author of a substantial amount of the material. But the traditions he used do have a long history within the order, some probably going back to Palestine.

5. The best available critical discussion of this work is by Paul Chandler, O. Carm., in "*Princeps et exemplar Carmelitarum*: The Prophet Elijah in the *Liber de Institutione primorum monachorum*," in *A Journey with Elijah*, ed. Paul Chandler, O. Carm. (Rome: Casa Editrice Institutum Carmelitanum, 1991), 111–134. Chandler has prepared a critical edition of the *Institution*.

6. *The Institution of the First Monks*, trans. Bryan Deschamp, O. Carm., in *Carmel in the World*, 13 (1974), 70. Deschamp's translation is used for chapters 1–9, or the first book of the *Institution*. For chapters 10–41, the remaining six books of the *Institution*, the translation used is Norman Werling, O. Carm., in *The Sword*, 4 (1940), 20–24, 152–160, 309–320; 5 (1941), 20–27, 131–139, 241–248; 6 (1942), 33–39, 147–155, 278–286; 7 (1943), 347–355. There are fifty-six chapters in the *Institution*, but the source used by Werling had reduced them to forty-one by excluding certain sources.

7. Deschamp, 71, 72.

8. Ibid., 75.

9. Ibid., 154.

10. Ibid., 156.

11. Ibid., 161.

12. Ibid., 248.

13. Ibid., 254.

14. Elijah was actually alone in Cherith, but the Carmelite reading sees him in a fraternal setting.

15. Werling, 5, 21.

16. It is possible the first book of the *Institution* was a separate work from a non-Carmelite source and Ribot would have had to explain the change of setting from Cherith to Mount Carmel. Cf. Chandler, 120.

17. Werling, 5, 135.

18. Ibid.

19. Ibid., 137. The *Institution* does not mention Elijah's flight into the desert after defeating the prophets of Baal. Chandler hypothesizes that the author did not want to acknowledge Elijah's frailty, a sensitive point in medieval literature. Cf. Chandler, 117, 118.

Notice that the author, surprisingly, does not identify the "gentle air" with a contemplative experience, which would seem to have been a natural interpretation for a Carmelite. Chandler theorizes that perhaps each locale in the Holy Land had its own traditions and those of Mount Carmel were different from the ones associated with Horeb. The Carmelites from the locale of Mount Carmel developed their own interpretations. If this is so, it is an argument for an early structuring, in Palestine, of the Carmelite tradition, which will then mature in Europe. Cf. Chandler, 119, 120.

20. Werling, 5, 138, 139.

21. Ibid., 243. "Elijah's eschatological role, his peace-bringing role assigned by God on Horeb, and the emphasis on the peaceful nature of the Mount Carmel community, make the theme of Elijah as a man of peace a prominent one in this work." Cf. Chandler, 122, 123.

22. Werling, 6, 34.

23. Ibid., 155.

24. Ibid.

25. Before the *Institution,* the Elijan and Marian traditions were two separate strands in the order, never satisfactorily integrated. Cf. Chandler, 117.

26. Ribot unites traditions about Mount Carmel, Elijah, and Mary under the rubric of virginity. Mount Carmel is understood to mean, under a false etymology, "knowledge of circumcision." Elijah and Mary are the first man and woman to practice voluntary virginity. Mary is the virgin who gives birth to the Messiah. Consequently, all three sources call the Carmelite to a purity of heart essential for a contemplative. Cf. Chandler, 117.

27. Werling, 6, 281.

28. Smet, 8.

29. Ibid., 21.

30. Ibid.

31. *Medieval Carmelite Heritage*, ed. Adrianus Staring, O. Carm. (Roma: Institutum Carmelitanum, 1989), 42. Trans. Christopher O'Donnell, O. Carm.

32. "Mary Mirrored in Our Rule: Baconthorpe's Commentary on the Rule," ed. Joachim Smet, O. Carm., in *The Sword*, 7 (February, 1943), 6–11.

33. *Analecta Ordinis Carmelitanum*, 15 (1950), 218.

34. Smet, 23.

35. Deschamp, 72.

Chapter Five

CONTEMPLATIVE PRAYER
Teresa of Avila and John of the Cross

The Institution of the First Monks had an important place in all the major reforms of the order. Its imagery and teaching deeply influenced the reform efforts of John Soreth, and the reform of Touraine as well. It is assumed John of the Cross studied the document since by his time it was mandated for all Carmelite novitiates. A Spanish copy of the *Institution* was available to Teresa in the convent of the Incarnation. Her challenge to her sisters conveys the spirit of this foundational myth:

> So I say now that all of us who wear this holy habit of Carmel are called to prayer and contemplation. This call explains our origin; we are descendants of men who felt this call, of those holy fathers on Mount Carmel who in such great solitude and contempt for the world sought this treasure, this precious pearl of contemplation that we are speaking about. Yet few of us dispose ourselves that the Lord may communicate it to us.[1]

Teresa's Castle Journey

Teresa of Avila's solution to fragmentation and dissipation was a healthy community life of moderate asceticism, with an emphasis on prayer. She wrote that the door to the inner castle, and therefore to true self-knowledge, was "prayer and reflection."[2]

Teresa defined prayer at one time as "nothing else than an

intimate sharing between friends."[3] But notice her assumption: in this prayer, our friend is the one who first speaks. The mystery at the center of the castle first "spoke" us into life, and continues to address us, calling us more deeply into our lives, into wider freedom, and more intimate union. We are, essentially, listeners for this voice, hearers of the Word. Prayer in the first instance, therefore, requires attentiveness. Initial efforts to pray may require great effort. Those people and things to which we have given our heart may be so preoccupying, so absorbing, that it is difficult to hear the "good shepherd with a whistle so gentle...."[4]

When she describes the process of a soul in prayer in her classic synthesis, *The Interior Castle*, Teresa begins by describing a person who may pray just a few times a month. She does not discount the value of this apparently minimal activity; she appreciates the difficulty involved in listening into one's life for more. She writes about the condition of this soul:

> Even though it may not be in a bad state it is so involved in worldly things and so absorbed with its possessions, honor, or business affairs, as I have said, that even though as a matter of fact it would want to see and enjoy its beauty these things do not allow it to; nor does it seem that it can slip free from so many impediments.[5]

The enemies of the soul at this point, Teresa observes, are fear, faint-heartedness, and cowardice. It is harder to hear a call than not to hear it. Or, where no one asks, no one need answer.

Where is the call coming from? From the center of ones' life. Teresa's image for the journey to and with God is the movement from the periphery of a circle to its center. We begin the pilgrimage living on the periphery of our lives, locked into many dissipating centers, and gradually, through prayer, we are de-centered and drawn to another Center. The advantage of Teresa's image is that God is not in the distance to be reached by crossing rivers, passing through deserts, or climbing mountains. God is "always already there" in the center of our existence. If anyone is absent from the relationship it is the human being who is unaware of the friendship being continually offered.

Where does one look to find God? Teresa points to many places of mediation: books, friends, times of illness, trials, moments in prayer. With regular attempts at prayer a person may progress to a point where the relationship with God becomes less generic and more personal. The one praying begins to realize that he or she is being personally addressed by God. This awareness is not necessarily more consoling; "...hearing His voice is a greater trial than not hearing it."[6]

Not only does it call for a response in one's life, but it throws light on various, up to now, dimly perceived corners of that life. The journey within the castle of one's life initially sounds like a peaceful setting aside of life's conflicts and entering the quiet sanctuary of an inner world. Teresa's experience shattered that hope. I went within, she reported, and I was at war with myself! The self-knowledge gained in prayer includes an awareness of our distance from God as well as the distance from our true self. The prayerful person may find herself ill at ease in her own house.

Teresa's Prayer

Teresa complained that she could not think much, nor could she imagine much. Sustained reflection with concluding resolutions was not the way her mind worked. Nor was she capable of spinning imaginative scenarios as a prayer form. She called her prayer a prayer of recollection.

> This is the method of prayer I then used: since I could not reflect discursively with the intellect, I strove to picture Christ within me, and it did me greater good–in my opinion–to picture Him in those scenes where I saw Him more alone. It seemed to me that being alone and afflicted, as a person in need, He had to accept me. I had many simple thoughts like these.[7]

She especially liked the scene in the garden of Gethsemane where, in her thoughts, she could remain alone with Christ. For many years, before going to bed, she briefly reflected upon this scene.

For many years, as well, she began her prayers by opening a book and using it to help her be aware of God's presence. Or, she said, she used flowers of the field, water, or other parts of creation. She said she looked at water more than anything else in her life. The important thing, she wrote, was not to think much but to love much. The book and the images helped her become aware of the presence of Christ. With that awareness she could enter into conversation or simply remain quiet with her Friend.

When writing for her sisters in the *Way of Perfection* Teresa encouraged them to represent the Lord close to them, at their side as their companion. "...Get used to this practice! Get used to it!"[8]

> I'm not asking you now that you think about Him or that you draw out a lot of concepts or make long and subtle reflections with your intellect. I'm not asking you to do anything more than look at Him....In the measure you desire Him, you will find Him.[9]

Teresa encouraged her women to honor their deeply felt responses to life. They need not hide their emotional state from the Lord. He is not like some husbands who expect their wives to be sad when they are sad and joyful when they are joyful. She assured her nuns that the Lord wants to accommodate himself to them:

> He submits to your will. If you are joyful, look at Him as risen. Just imagining how He rose from the tomb will bring you joy. The brilliance! The beauty! The majesty! How victorious!
>
> ...If you are experiencing trials or are sad, behold Him on the way to the garden: what great affliction He bore in His soul;...Or behold Him bound to the column, filled with pain....Or behold Him burdened with the cross, for they didn't even let Him take a breath.[10]

In this meeting of moods, each rejoices with the other, each consoles the other in their sorrow. The one praying is not reducing the Lord to the dimensions of her life, but she is placing her own responses to life in a broader context. She is reading her life *through* the life of Christ. In the relationship she finds Christ available to her, for affirmation as well as for challenge.

Teresa's own prayer experiences taught her to trust the realization that Christ desired her. In her life within the convent and in her dealings with society outside the convent she had been looking for affirmation, for a sense of being wanted. Her prayer relationship with Christ eventually impressed her with the fact that she had been desired all along. She realized that the challenge was not to earn God's affirmation; acceptance and affirmation had always been offered her. The challenge was to meet Christ's acceptance of her, to accept the acceptance.

But the relationship with Christ all rests on a sense of his presence, and communication with this companion on our life's journey. The ever practical Teresa advises her nuns to become aware of this presence by using "a good book written in the vernacular." And, "try to carry about an image or painting of this Lord that is to your liking, not so as to carry it about on your heart and never look at it but so as to speak often with Him; for He will inspire you with what to say."[11]

The Problem of the Good, Adult Christian

Even a well-ordered prayer life can eventually be its own enemy. When Teresa describes the situation of someone who is in the third dwelling place of the castle, she describes a Christian who prays regularly, practices asceticism, is generous in sharing goods with the needy. This person's life is well-balanced and moderated. Other people ask this person for guidance in their spiritual journey.

By the time Teresa finishes describing this prayerful person one would think the goal, the center of the castle, had been reached. Why is this only the third of seven dwelling places? Teresa hints at the problem. These people are so balanced, she observed, that you do not have to worry about them going to extremes in anything. She describes their life as "well-ordered," "well-structured."

It becomes obvious that the very security of this situation and the sense of well-being which accompanies it have now become blocks to further penetration of other inner rooms. Having responded well to God by establishing a disciplined, prayerful, generous life, the very control itself has become the latest attachment. Further growth will call for the return of insecurity and the lessening of control. Having become quite free in their availability to God, these people can still move into wider realms of freedom. Their prayer needs to become more contemplative, their listening more sensitive and attuned, their grasp of their lives more relaxed and open-handed.

Teresa uses an image to describe the difference between prayer that is largely the graced outcome of our own efforts, and prayer which seems unrelated to our efforts and appears to have its source elsewhere. The image is a description of two ways of filling a fountain. One way is the laborious process of pulling up water from a distant well and transporting it by aqueduct to the fountain. The other way is to have the fountain over the source of the water, filling up effortlessly from within. The first way is similar to our efforts to meditate; the second way pictures a prayer which has become more contemplative.

The consolations of the first way of praying begin in our efforts and end in God. We have genuine enjoyment, contentment, happiness, but it may be constricting; we cling to it, not wanting to lose it. The spiritual delight accompanying a more contemplative prayer begins in God, as it were, and ends in us. It amplifies our spirits rather than constricts them. God at the center of one's life is overflowing into the heart.

The purpose of prayer, Teresa regularly reminds us, is conformity with God's will, not experiences of consolation or delight. Teresa realizes that not everyone will be able to report such experiences, especially some of the more ecstatic experiences she had. It does not mean they are not growing in their relationship with Christ. If their lives are more and more in conformity with God's will, if they gradually learn to want what God wants, and this desire is expressed in the way they live, then the journey through the castle is leading to a fruitful union.

Contemplative Prayer

Just how one transitions from meditation to contemplation, or incorporates contemplative prayer within more meditative prayer is a subject with which Teresa struggles. On the one hand, she holds that contemplation is pure gift; one cannot prepare for or summon it. This gift from God is totally gratuitous, coming and going according to patterns unrelated to our activity.

On the other hand, she does acknowledge that we can make ourselves more open to such prayer. She is critical of any unilateral effort on our part to stop using our natural abilities to reflect and imagine in order to be more "contemplative." She does, however, recommend slowing down our normal processes, keeping the mind from wandering by reciting a few simple words. "And without any effort or noise," she advises, "the soul should strive to cut down the rambling of the intellect–but not suspend either it or the mind; it is good to be aware that one is in God's presence and of who God is."[12] In time the words may fall away in the pure receptivity of contemplation. The person in the third dwelling places, then, is encouraged to quiet the busyness of their religious activity, to slow down the tight wording of their life, to loosen control and give God's spirit room to breathe new life.

The stillness of contemplation will never be such that we no longer have use of ordinary means of praying, much less that we no longer need the gospels. Teresa was revolted by teaching which held that contemplative prayer eventually superseded meditation on the gospels and participation in the ritual life of the church. Her emphatic teaching was that we never get beyond our need for the humanity of Christ and the celebrations of the church. Life is long, she said, don't just sit there in an attempt to force or simulate contemplation.

> ...Someone must necessarily blow on the fire so that heat will be given off. Would it be good for a soul with this dryness to wait for fire to come down from heaven to burn this sacrifice that it is making of itself to God, as did our Father Elijah? No, certainly not, nor is it right to expect miracles....But His Majesty...desires that we help ourselves in every way possible.[13]

Different ways of praying have their seasons and the seasons have their natural rhythms. She was convinced that even simple vocal prayers are sufficient to open one to the gift of contemplation.

This prayerful listening to a deeper center within her life slowly freed Teresa from the many fragmenting centers around which her life revolved. Listening to the call, and responding to it, eroded the attachments which had confined her heart. That which she could not remove through sheer willpower slowly melted away in the new relationship nurtured in prayer. The only truly terminal problem was to stop praying.

Theologian Monica Hellwig aptly summarized Teresa's message: a faithful and perduring attentiveness to our depths and center is the best cooperation we can give to God who is reorienting our life.[14] In other words, if we give God our attention, God will draw our whole being into proper focus.

John of the Cross

John of the Cross taught that contemplation was the key to freeing a heart enslaved by idols. John has a reputation in the history of spirituality for rugged asceticism, but actually at the core of his teaching is an acknowledgment that only God's love can break through the heart wrapped in attachments. Contemplation is simply opening one's life to this love.

John certainly counseled disciplined efforts. For example, in *The Ascent of Mount Carmel* (Book 1, chapter 13) he offered a series of counsels which would help free a heart.[15] He begins by urging the imitation of Christ by bringing one's life into conformity with his. Then he says this imitation of Christ would be accomplished by the renunciation of any sensory satisfaction that was not "purely for the honor and glory of God." He follows this challenging counsel with a series of maxims, such as: "Endeavor to be inclined always not to the easiest but to the most difficult...." In addition he encourages the reader to "act with contempt for yourself and desire that all others do likewise." John concludes with a string of verses which are variations on the theme, "To come to possess all, desire the possession of nothing." This one chapter in *The Ascent of Mount Carmel* is enough to substantiate John's ascetical reputation in the church.

However, to be preoccupied with the intensity and challenges of his counsels is to miss a central point in John's teaching. In the very next chapter (chapter 14) he admits that his counsels, by themselves, are bound to fail. No amount of ascetical effort can free a heart from its attachments if the heart has nowhere to go. The heart cannot break away from whatever is providing some life, some meaning and happiness, and go into an affective vacuum, and there await a better offer. It is an impossible task, John concludes. No ascetical regimen, no controlled, disciplined effort by itself can wrestle a person's life into submission. The solution is contemplation.

Only when a stronger, deeper love is kindled in the heart can it let go of its lesser loves. Only when a flame is kindled which lures the person past the attachments will the soul release its grasp on whatever has been so transfixing. When that trust grows, then those things which had captured the heart begin to fall away. What could not be thawed ascetically, begins to melt away in the warmth of God's love. It is mysticism, the experience of being grasped by God's love, which allows asceticism, a disciplined response to this love. Attending to that flame and following its allure is contemplative activity. John writes:

> Accordingly, the moment prayer begins, the soul, as one with a store of water, drinks peaceably without the labor and the need to fetch the water through the channels of past considerations, forms, and figures. The moment it recollects itself in the presence of God it enters into an act of general, loving, peaceful, and

> tranquil knowledge, drinking wisdom and love and delight.[16]

In *The Living Flame of Love,* John further comments on this experience:

> Since God, then, as the giver communes with individuals through a simple, loving knowledge, they also, as the receivers, commune with God through a simple and loving knowledge of attention, so knowledge is thus joined with knowledge and love with love.[17]

John remembers a scene from scripture, and his Carmelite heritage: "...some theologians think our Father Elijah saw God in the whistling of the gentle breeze heard on the mount at the mouth of his cave [1 Kgs 19:11–13]."[18]

Dark Nights

It is from this Carmelite tradition that the haunting image of the dark night of the soul emerges in the church. The image is taken from a poem of John of the Cross which captures his experience of God while in prison: "One dark night...," it begins.

John went on to comment on this poem, and this image. He said it spoke of times when God's love was so opaque that it could not be seen or felt. As a matter of fact, there are times when God's love seems to be over against us, negating us. John gave signs for judging whether our experience is truly from God: when one is finding no satisfaction or meaning whether in religion or in any other area of life; when one has a sense of guilt, feels responsible for these doldrums, wishes the former sense of satisfaction could be restored, but can do nothing about it; when a person's normal problem-solving approach of thinking, analyzing, and deciding no longer works, and prayer goes quiet.

When these signs are present, wrote John, one is in a loving condition. God's love is healing the soul and freeing it. There is nothing in the love which is painful or dark. But, because of the healings we need, the love is dark and, at times, painful to us. In time the confusion and pain lift, and consolation is restored.

When life and prayer dry up this way, John recommends entering into this dark experience. He warns against forcing more understanding and control into this situation. It is not a time for making secure, but for taking a chance and letting go. John recommends entering into this dark time with patience, perseverance, and trust. For a while one may have no words, no thoughts, no solutions. John urges that we go quiet, and prepare to endure as long as need be. In the quiet, dark time John counsels having an attitude of "loving attentiveness." At this time we are a watch in the night, alert to the approach of God. In time, a sense of presence replaces our loneliness, meaning replaces our confusion, and once again we are able to word our lives.

John wrote about even more difficult times in life when life's journey itself is called into question. John speaks of a midnight time in life, a dark night of the spirit. One's sins and weaknesses press in and undermine any sense of worth. Life's limitations are painfully experienced. Anxiety and bitterness spread through the soul. The fundamental trust in life's promises and one's own worth has evaporated and now no one and nothing is trustworthy. The soul experiences an intense loneliness, feeling abandoned by all; even God seems to be walking away, perhaps in anger and rejection. Prayer is all but impossible.

Thérèse of Lisieux, the popular saint of our time, experienced an intense night of the spirit in her final illness; the darkness mocked even her belief in an afterlife.[19] The potential unbeliever lurking in the heart of every believer is given free rein to question the very purpose of life. Does anyone or anything promise the fulfillment of the deepest desires of our hearts? Or are we meant to have those desires frustrated, mocked, by a life which simply blazes for a brief period of time between two vast darknesses?

At the heart of the experience, one way or another the fear is that I have lost God, and all that God means to human existence. The dark night of the spirit is John's expression for the deeply unsettling experience of one's sinfulness, the finiteness of the human condition, and God's transcendence.

John counsels against prematurely solving this condition. A deep purifying and healing is going on under the impact of God's love. No words, explanations, counsels, or plans can help. Indeed, John says, it is time to "put one's mouth in the dust," and proceed with a naked faith. The only answer is the answer of Jesus on the cross: to trust in the sometimes dark love of God.

This powerful image, and John's reflection and recommendations regarding this experience, have been a great, consoling, contribution to the Christian journey. Just when one might be tempted to turn back, either for fear of having taken the wrong path or because the cost is too high, this tradition testifies to the benefits of continuing on in deep faith.

It is a tradition that tells us not to be afraid of the dark, of apparent failure. It encourages us to have trust even in the face of our own sinfulness, our own inauthenticity. Let nothing have the last word, except the God whose word to us is forgiveness, peace, welcome. The log, initially scarred by fire, slowly becomes one with the flames.

Pope John Paul II, an ardent student of John of the Cross, observed that the image of the dark night fittingly captures the suffering of our world:

> Our age has known times of anguish which have made us understand this expression better and which have furthermore given it a kind of collective character. Our age speaks of the silence or absence of God. It has known so many calamities, so much suffering inflicted by wars and by the destruction of so many innocent beings. The term *dark night* is now used of all of life and not just of a phase of the spiritual journey. The Saint's doctrine is now invoked in response to this unfathomable mystery of human suffering.
>
> I refer to this *specific world of suffering* ....Physical, moral and spiritual suffering, like sickness—like the plagues of hunger, like war, injustice, solitude, the lack of meaning in life, the very fragility of human existence, the sorrowful knowledge of sin, the seeming

absence of God—are for the believer all purifying experiences which might be called *night of faith.*

To this experience St. John of the Cross has given the symbolic and evocative name *dark night,* and he makes it refer explicitly to the light and obscurity of the mystery of faith. He does not try to give to the appalling problem of suffering an answer in the speculative order; but in the light of the Scripture and of experience he discovers and sifts out something of the marvelous transformation which God effects in the darkness, since "He knows how to draw good from evil so wisely and beautifully" (*Cant.* B 23:5). In the final analysis, we are faced with living the mystery of death and resurrection in Christ in all truth.[20]

The Carmelite Contribution

Carmel in the contemporary church stands for prayer. The original Carmelites and the saints of Carmel, known and unknown, were preoccupied with attentiveness to Mystery. From this attentiveness flowed identity, community, and service of the world. If the tradition of Carmel has anything to say to the modern world it is a word about prayer.

The Rule of Carmel, a quilt of scriptural references, focused the Carmelite on God's Word. Listening to scripture read in common, praying the psalms together, meditating on scripture in the silence of their cells, were fundamental prayer activities of the early Carmelites, and remain privileged forms of communication with God in prayer.[21]

There is no Carmelite method of prayer, only the encouragement to pray. Alone or with others, the presence of God is the foundational reality, the horizon against which our human activity takes place. Consciously attending to that foundation, that horizon, opens us to a full life. Carmelites pray with many forms, but essentially all forms are meant to open us to the Mystery which haunts our lives.

In seeking God, Carmelites discovered that God had been

pursuing them in love. Their very seeking and desiring was a response to a shepherd's whistle so gentle as to be almost imperceptible. In following the call they found themselves in a loving relationship; they were desired, affirmed, wanted by God.

Teresa of Avila concluded that God does not wait until we get our life in order. God meets us where we are and asks us to trust that acceptance. After all, Teresa wrote, Jesus did not wait until the Samaritan woman straightened out her life before he spoke with her at the well. Teresa said she probably should not have called her autobiography "the story of my life," but instead, "the story of God's mercies."

John of the Cross learned that God's love had to lead the way before a heart truly became free. On its own, the heart is not going to let go of whatever is providing some meaning, some happiness, some fulfillment of desire, even if it has become enslaved; only when God kindles in a soul a deeper love which lures us past our other loves will we be able to open our hands and relax our grasp on our lives. Teresa taught that the important thing was not to think much but to love much; John taught that desiring God is the beginning of possessing God.

John gives no methods or approaches to prayer; any and all are suitable to open us to God's presence, but none of them should take God's place. "One rosary is no more influential with God than is another."[22] Where there is faith, any image suffices; where there is no faith, no image suffices.

He encouraged a silent attentiveness to where our heart is struggling and experiencing exhaustion. In the night no method or solution is at hand other than patience, perseverance, and trust. Carmelites learned in contemplation that we all are poor in spirit and have to wait in hope for God's mercy.

Thérèse of Lisieux, too, learned in prayer that "It's all grace." She entered Carmel with heroic ideals and realized they were unattainable. She often slept during prayer time. Her only hope was to trust in God's mercy and grace, and to live with the utter abandonment and confidence of a child playing in the company of a parent. It is a "little way" not simply because she did ordinary things in place of heroic efforts, but because nothing big or small was needed to please God.

Thérèse had the best of models, but she found her own way. Even though Teresa of Avila was her patron and the writings of John of the Cross nourished her, they pointed her to Jesus:

> Ah! how many lights have I not drawn from the Works of our holy Father, St. John of the Cross! At the ages of seventeen and eighteen I had no other spiritual nourishment; later on, however, all books left me in aridity and I'm still in that state....It is especially the Gospels which sustain me during my hours of prayer....
>
> Jesus has no need of books or teachers to instruct souls; He teaches without the noise of words. Never have I heard Him speak, but I feel that He is within me at each moment; He is guiding and inspiring me with what I must say and do.[23]

Thérèse learned that the secret of her life and vocation was not that she was worthy but that God freely *chose* her. She quoted St. Paul: "So it depends not on human will or exertion, but on God who shows mercy" (Rom 9:16).

Brother Lawrence of the Resurrection, a Carmelite whose simple encouragements to remember the presence of God are well known, described his own prayer:

> My commonest attitude is this simple attentiveness, an habitual, loving turning of my eyes to God, to whom I often find myself bound with more happiness and gratification than that which a babe enjoys clinging to its nurse's breast. So, if I dare use this expression, I should be glad to describe this condition as "the breasts of God," for the inexpressible happiness I savour and experience there.[24]

Once one is in the presence of this friend, is attentive to this friend, then prayer takes its course. I may simply listen as this friend speaks through the urgings of my heart, the thoughts of my mind, the objects and people in the world around me. Teresa of Avila counseled, "...He wants us to ask creatures who it is who made them...."[25] I can be quiet and mull what I have heard. I can take inventory of my life in the presence of this one who loves me. I can speak about my needs and concerns. I can make present in this meeting my loved ones, parents, enemies. I can speak from a heart overflowing with gratitude. I can simply be still. In prayer there is nothing I have to accomplish, but simply stay open to the love of a graciousness at the core of life. John of the Cross was able to write, "How gently and lovingly you wake in my heart...."[26]

Perhaps the most difficult thing for a Christian is to truly accept the fact that he or she is loved by God. As a statement, God's love for us is easy to acknowledge. As a basis on which to proceed in trust, the fact that God loves us is problematic. This gratuitous love is the basis for our Christian living. And it is at the heart of the Carmelite experience. Contemplation, or an openness to God's transforming love, no matter how it is approaching, is the only solid basis for proceeding in life. And contemplation is the only sure antidote, the "solution" to a life given to fragmentation and idolatry.

NOTES

1. Teresa of Avila, *The Interior Castle,* in *The Collected Works of St. Teresa of Avila*, 2, trans. Kieran Kavanaugh, O.C.D., and Otilio Rodriguez, O.C.D. (Washington, D.C.: ICS Publications, 1980), The Fifth Dwelling Places, chap. 1, no. 2.
2. Ibid., The First Dwelling Places, chap. 1, no. 7.
3. *The Book of Her Life* in *The Collected Works,* 1, chap. 8, no. 5.
4. *The Interior Castle*, The Fourth Dwelling Places, chap. 3, no. 2.
5. Ibid., The First Dwelling Places, chap. 2, no. 14.
6. Ibid., The Second Dwelling Places, chap. 1, no. 2.
7. *The Book of Her Life*, chap. 9, no. 4.
8. *The Way of Perfection* in *The Collected Works*, 2, chap. 26, no. 2.
9. Ibid., no. 3.
10. Ibid., nos. 4, 5.
11. Ibid., no. 9.

12. *The Interior Castle*, The Fourth Dwelling Places, chap. 3, no. 7.

13. Ibid., The Sixth Dwelling Places, chap. 7, no. 8.

14. Monica Hellwig, "St. Teresa's Inspiration for Our Times," in *Carmelite Studies*, vol. 3, 214, 215.

15. John of the Cross, *The Ascent of Mount Carmel*, in *The Collected Works of St. John of the Cross*. trans. Kieran Kavanaugh, O.C.D., and Otilio Rodriguez, O.C.D. (Washington, D.C.: ICS Publications, 1991), Book 1, chap. 13.

16. Ibid., Book 2, chap. 14, no. 2.

17. John of the Cross, *The Living Flame of Love* in *The Collected Works*, stanza 3, no. 34.

18. John of the Cross, *The Spiritual Canticle* in *The Collected Works*, stanzas 14 and 15, no. 14.

19. Popularly known as the Little Flower, Thérèse (1873–1897) entered the Discalced Carmel of Lisieux, France, at the age of fifteen and died of tuberculosis at age twenty-four. Her autobiography is a warm, faith-filled account which sees God's presence and love in her life even in times of darkness and suffering.

20. *Master in the Faith*. Apostolic Letter of John Paul II in *Walking Side by Side with All Men and Women* (Rome: Institutum Carmelitanum, 1991), 22, 23.

21. Carlos Mesters, O. Carm., has identified steps in a process of *lectio divina*, a prayerful reading of scripture:

1. Opening prayer, an invocation of the Holy Spirit.
2. Slow and attentive reading of the text.
3. A moment of interior silence to recall what I have read.
4. Look at the meaning of each phrase.
5. Bring that Word into the present, ponder it, in relation to my life.
6. Broaden my vision by relating this text to other biblical texts.
7. Read the text again, prayerfully, giving a response to God.
8. Formulate my commitment in life.
9. Pray with a suitable psalm.
10. Choose a phrase which captures the meaning and memorize it.

This process may be adapted for group reading of, and reflection on, scripture as well. Mesters observes that the communities of the poor in Latin America have been using a form of *lectio divina* as they read their lives through the Word of God, and the Word of God through their lives. Cf. Mesters, "The Carmelite Rule and the Reading of the Bible," in *Carmelite Charism* (Melbourne: Carmelite Communications, 1991), 38, 39.

22. John of the Cross, *The Ascent of Mount Carmel,* 3, in *The Collected Works,* chap. 35, no. 7.

23. Thérèse of Lisieux, *The Story of A Soul,* trans. John Clarke, O.C.D. (Washington, D.C.: ICS Publications, 1976), 179.

24. Brother Lawrence, *The Practice of the Presence of God,* trans. E.M. Blaiklock (Nashville: Thomas Nelson, Inc., 1981), 45. Lawrence (1614–1691) left the military to become a cook with the Discalced Carmelites. Abbé de Beaufort posthumously published a collection of Lawrence's sayings and letters.

25. Teresa of Avila, *The Interior Castle,* The Sixth Dwelling Places, chap. 7, no. 9.

26. John of the Cross, "The Living Flame of Love," in *The Collected Works*, stanza 4.

Chapter Six

PRAYER AND THE SELF

Issues in Human Development

The contemplative emphasis in the Carmelite tradition implies living with greater awareness, a wider consciousness. The goal of prayer is not to become isolated in a corner but engaged in life, one's own and the life of the world. A life lived without the attentive listening of prayer is often a life lived quite unconsciously. As Carl Jung wrote, "Where no one asks, no one need answer."

We may assume that some of the first Carmelites arrived on Mount Carmel only after having undergone serious personality changes, the result of what we today would call transitions or passages. In their homelands where they grew up they would have formed their basic identity. They would have entered into responsible relationships, perhaps deeply loving relationships. Some of them may have been quite well known in their communities; they may have been leaders.

What events and decisions brought them to a remote place on a mountain ridge far from their homes can only be imagined. Dark nights and thoroughgoing conversions may have been the prelude for some of the men. On the mountain they sought conditions which would support their growing commitments and further their spiritual development. They probably would have simply said that life on the mountain was their way of following Christ.

Today we understand that prayer also activates powers of the psyche, and personality is opened to its hidden depths. If we assume that our unlived lives, our depths, are first met outside us in some symbolic form, then even the living conditions of the early Carmelites may have been expressive of their interiority, and, ideally, fostered greater interiority. The cluster of huts and caves on Mount Carmel provided the first Carmelites with an environment conducive to attentiveness to God and, most probably, had profound impact on their psychological well-being.

The first articles of their Rule addressed the physical and structural conditions which would allow them live out their allegiance to Jesus Christ.[1] Each was to have a separate dwelling letting the lie of the land dictate its location. The individual Carmelite was urged to stay in or near his cell, ruminating on scripture, unless occupied elsewhere. They were to elect and obey a leader, a prior, whose dwelling was to be at the entrance of the wadi. There, the prior would be the first to meet those who approached the site. The individuality of each person, and that person's unique relationship with God, was honored and protected in the physical arrangements of the first community of Carmelites.

The architecture of the wadi expressed the fundamental conviction of the Carmelites that God was the center of their existence, the guarantee of their personhood. Albert, the Rule-giver, prescribed that they should build an oratory, a small chapel, somewhere in the middle of their huts and caves. In this space they gathered daily to celebrate the death and resurrection of Jesus and to renew their commitment to their common project. On Sundays they discussed their life together, correcting and encouraging one another, giving voice to the values which drew them to the mountain. The oratory in the center of the wadi expressed the sacred center of human life. In contact with that center the Carmelites found their identity and were formed into a community.

The Rule of Carmel situates the Carmelite in a place of solitude and of silence. This solitude and silence allow the Mystery at the center of all lives to emerge. The chaos of life gives way to a cosmos ordered by God's self-communication. Far from isolation and non-communication, the prescriptions to spend time alone and to work in silence created in the wadi conditions of alert listening. The sight of the sea at the mouth of the canyon, the feel of the breezes blowing in from the Mediterranean, the shapes created by the contours of the wadi, are among the impressions even today which fill the senses. In these conditions, while he prayed and worked, the Carmelite listened for a gentle whistle, a silent sound, an awakening in the heart. More than a physical silence, the silence urged by the Rule was meant to permeate the hermit's interiority so that his whole being became an expectancy, an awaiting. God is met and disoriented psychic structures find a healing.

Attentiveness to Presence at the center has become an enduring Carmelite activity. The door to the castle of our souls and its center is prayer and reflection, wrote Teresa. John of the Cross urged that we become a watch in the night, listening for God's approach. When our words fail, meaning evaporates, and a remorseful guilt overtakes us, John counseled quiet, and, in the quiet, a "loving attentiveness." Love is at work.

Self-knowledge

The writings of Teresa of Avila and John of the Cross demonstrate psychological subtlety. Without having our contemporary categories, they nonetheless were able to convey a nuanced understanding of human development. Teresa used rich imagery to express the realities of the psyche.[2] John wrote poetry, amplified it with scriptural imagery, and developed his thought in scholastic categories. He used the psychological framework available to him, a faculty psychology, to express the impact of God's love on his personality structure.[3]

Teresa believed that self-knowledge was essential for spiritual development. Through self-knowledge we come to know God. On the other hand, the self is only truly known in relationship to God. When she could most fully say "God," she could most fully say "Teresa." The self-knowledge she gained was a knowledge of her essential poverty yet her immense worth based on God's grace and mercy.

This knowledge would include knowledge of inner fragmentation, compulsions, addictions which distort the heart. These realities float into awareness as prayer loosens layers of the psyche. Deeper union with God was not always pleasant for Teresa because of the greater awareness accompanying her prayer. When she writes her autobiography, she describes an adolescence which seems seriously irresponsible; but it is an adolescence viewed through the self-awarenesss of a fifty-year-old.

John of the Cross believed that when a personality is not centered on God, but is centered on some part of God's creation, the personality is dysfunctional. When the true center emerges, false centers die, and the personality heals. From this center a person hears his or her name more clearly than ever before; and other people are valued as brothers and sisters. John learned that true community is formed when each one is related, not only to the others, but most especially to the Mystery at the center of all lives.

Prayer offers an opportunity to hear parts of the self which have not been allowed room at the banquet table of our life. Without a deep listening to one's life and to God in prayer, our unlived life is met outside us in projection. Our life and our gods are all outside. We then live with false selves and false gods. A greater openness to God results in greater self-appropriation, a necessity before one can truly lose oneself.

If the world around us holds for us the secrets within us, then a contemplative attentiveness to this world may reveal our inner life. Teresa encouraged her readers to let creatures speak of their maker. And she observed that there is more to every little thing, even the tiniest ant. Her symbolic attitude allows access to the mystery of God and to the equally mysterious self. Teresa often knew that activity was taking place deep within her psyche in prayer, even though on the surface her mind could not focus on prayer.

Carmelites have developed a particularly expressive language for the soul. The place of the order's founding, and the architecture and atmosphere of the wadi became the first words of the spiritual tradition of Carmel. The hermits found in scripture a language which gave words to the Mystery that dwelt with them in their cells. *The Institution of the First Monks* wove a narrative based on Carmel's relationship to the prophet Elijah and to Mary, and through story expressed the ascetical-mystical ideal of the Carmelites. The "land of Carmel" became symbolic of an inner terrain where the human spirit enacted a love story with

God. The poetry of John of the Cross, the lively writing of Teresa of Avila, the tender expressiveness of Thérèse of Lisieux added to Carmel's thesaurus. Contemporary pilgrims may find in the tradition of Carmel a primordial wording of their soul's adventure.

Ego

To have an ego, in our contemporary society, is often understood in a pejorative sense. In human development, the emergence of an ego is an important and necessary occurrence. It is only the ego out of touch with the rest of the self which begins to distort the personality and life around it.

Initially, the ego is a tentative and fragile development in the unfolding of personality. The infant is born with a vast psychic inheritance, an inner cosmos, out of which the ego is shaped. The development of the ego is a graced freeing of ego from the grip of the unconscious, from anonymity, from collectivity, from merely instinctual living. The spirituality of ego development supports a movement into consciousness where an identity is slowly forged, relationships are developed, values are interiorized, and a world view is formed. This day of development is a prelude to any talk of "dark nights."

The ego arrives at the noontime of life in full stride. However, it is just at that point when deep reversals are beginning to take place within the psyche. Inevitably the development of the first part of life reaches a dead end, because, as Jung observed, it is necessarily one-sided. Too much of personality has remained untapped.[4] This unlived life lives on in the unconscious like glowing coals, waiting to burst into flames. Neglected sources of life begin to seek an expression in the conscious personality, demanding that ego-consciousness widen to make room for the new life. But ego has often reached a petrified state and the new life must force its way into awareness. Ego is often the last to recognize what is happening. And yet, it is the ego's destiny to house these conflicts, to be the theater in which the story of personality is played out.

Much of the literature of the Carmelites assaults the ego. The Rule forces it to simplify, to disengage from distraction, and to focus. Owning nothing and told to merge with the land, ego loses footholds where security might have been found. It is to live in an undefended manner, obeying a leader, open to criticism and correction from others. The Rule and the lifestyle it urges invites ego to let go of its firm grasp on the personality and on life, and to embark on a sometimes painful journey. Ego is asked to stand ready to hear if there are other voices in the house of personality.[5]

Ego is asked to identify with Elijah in the *Institution of the First Monks*. The key scriptural text in the first part of that document is 1 Kings 17:3–4 where the word of the Lord tells Elijah to depart and go eastward to the brook Cherith, and there he is to drink of the brook, and the ravens will feed him. The medieval Carmelite heard in this command the ascetical and mystical ideal of Carmel. From a developmental point of view, ego must leave its position of preeminence and with docility embark on a journey not of its own making. It is told to let go of its anchors and follow, not lead. The journey is difficult as it works against its selfish, sinful habits, and takes up residence in a life supportive of others' well-being, a life of charity. Ego is asked to trust in the promise that through it all there will be nourishment and even greater life.

The Carmelites testify that the outcome of prayer is humility. In the process the ego is often bruised but should emerge the better for the experience. Some of the stronger language of John of the Cross could be understood as even advocating annihilation of the ego. He was sensitively aware of the ego's fear and distrust, and its tendency to close in upon itself. The annihilation of the ego, however, is never the goal. It is this soul's destiny to discover itself in relationship with God at its center. The ego necessarily plays a major role in this privileged encounter.

The problem is not ego, but an egocentric life. It is the ego which lives in isolation from the deeper, nourishing sources of the psyche that becomes a problem to itself, to others, and which distorts God. The ego that rests in its own knowledge and control is not aware of the psychic forces which can undermine its position. The beginner John of the Cross describes in the *Dark Night* (Book One, Chapters 2 to 8) is a good person, but one basically unaware of the selfishness hidden within the apparent virtues. When John of the Cross describes the effects of contemplative prayer he is not describing an annihilation of the ego but a repositioning of the ego in reference to the self, to God and to others.[6] Ego is now acutely aware of its selfish and sinful tendencies. Reverence has been restored to the personality which had grown presumptuous. The person, the ego, now takes its place in the circle of humanity, and no longer judges. Once-proud ego is now able to say "we poor."

Paradoxically, the surrender results in an awareness of a deeper foundation for one's life. The ego is not annihilated but is put in touch with enlivening sources of life, sources received as gracious gift. The humility arising from this process results in an even surer, more confident ego. The person is able to proceed not on the basis of assumed strengths, but with a realization of a giftedness offered it from beyond its own feeble powers. A life is seen now not as the story of an individual's strengths and weaknesses, but as a story of God's mercy.

In Teresa's own life this deeper humility coincided with energetic, effective efforts to reform the Carmelite Order by establishing new communities. Humility, for her, obviously did not mean shrinking from life. As a matter of fact she warned that a humility which led to a poor self-image was one of the greatest temptations of the devil.

In much of the literature of the Carmelites there is a confident tone as they report their experiences and insights. The experience of God has softened any arrogance, but also allows them to write with a conviction, even while protesting their faithlessness. Teresa complains about her feminine nature and its limitations, yet she is also convinced that her writing will be beneficial to readers, and she is willing to fight for her convictions even in the face of opposition from more learned figures of her day.[7]

True humility resulting from prayer is an acknowledgment that our ego is not the center of the personality, much less the center of the world. It is an acceptance of the truth of things. We are not our own cause nor do we have the strength to guarantee our lives in any way. The ego is forced to acknowledge its poverty of spirit. In this acceptance there is a self-transcendence, a true losing of oneself. The ego learns to surrender the personality to another center, a psychological center and also a transcendent Mystery at the core of its existence.

Persona

One of the important tasks in the first part of life is to develop a healthy persona, a way of presenting oneself to the world. A healthy persona balances one's own self-expectations, the expectations of others, and the very real possibilities of one's personality. The persona is a mediator between the ego and the outer world. That outer world, or collective consciousness, is a powerful shaping force for a persona. We learn to see ourselves through others' eyes and speak with others' voices. A challenge for the ego is to step out from behind the masks or personae it is wearing and to find its own voice; a persona eventually becomes inadequate and will have to become more flexible, perhaps only after an initial disintegration.

The Carmelite inclination to go apart, into real deserts or simply into one's interior desert, manifests an uneasiness with personae, or being part of a collective. Often the very geography and living conditions chosen by early Carmelites was an effort to free themselves from society's expectations. The phrase they used, *vacare deo* (to be free for God), captures something of the intent.

In the renewal of their lives, the first Carmelites often had to set aside family and societal expectations in order to enter on a pilgrimage to the land of the gospel. They went to the edges of society and the church. As part of their new identity they took on the role of penitent, pilgrim, hermit. As a sign of their radical change they rejected existing rules, and requested a new formula for living. Their Rule encouraged them to put on the armor of God, a new persona, letting faith be their shield and holy thoughts their constant reminder.

The ego has to thread its way between the collective consciousness of society and the collective depths of the psyche. Too much societal identification and one sees oneself only through the eyes of others. One begins to live solely in the persona, losing touch with the rest of the personality. Too much unconscious identification and one can become inflated, claiming for oneself powers which rightfully belong to the "gods." An inauthentic prophet blindly takes on an archetypal role and in her hubris brings about societal and personal destruction.

The Carmelite heritage of prophecy, beginning with the major figure of Elijah, demands a certain distancing from societal values in order to present a critique. It also is the result of a contemplative prayer which opens the personality to God's invitation. In the experience of John of the Cross, the contemplative is led into a "vast wilderness" where one's former identity and value system is left behind. Here a new knowing, now by "unknowing," takes place. From this stance the contemplative is able to offer a critique of society as well as the church. In its own history, Carmel has known the sharp critique of its contemplatives. The prophetic cannot be a persona seized, but a role taken on reluctantly. Elijah understands himself as the only one left to defend the true God. Contemplative prayer is not seen as inimical to justice and peace concerns. On the contrary, the contemplative is expected to be one who sees the reality of a situation.

In Teresa's day the concept of "honor" greatly shaped the persona. Honor was the mask through which one related to society. It shaped one's self-understanding and affected one's relationships. Teresa was particularly sensitive to the confines of such a persona and its deleterious effect on a gospel-oriented life. Her communities were to function in such a way that only God's honor was served. But even that noble intention may lead to rigidity.

The soul traveling through Teresa's inner castle slowly takes on the persona of a good religious person, one who has established a life structure which would be in accord with their own self-understanding and the expectations of others. As good as it is, the very security of the lifestyle becomes the latest attachment which hinders the soul from moving through the castle.

Continued attentive prayer with an openness to being led, may result in transformations of the persona. How one understands oneself and how one presents oneself to the world around may undergo change. Carl Jung believed that ego often will not be willing to explore other rooms in the psyche until the persona begins to disintegrate.[8] This disintegration may happen when the persona is no longer adequate to express new life emerging from within the personality or expected by others.

The temptation is to wrap one's persona even more tightly around oneself. Taking even greater control of one's life, and refusing to hear any questioning of that life, ego identifies even more tightly with persona and cuts off potentially nourishing sources from within the unconscious. Just as the early Carmelites had to let go the security of the wadi on Mount Carmel for the unknown challenges of Europe, so the dweller of the third dwelling place in the castle needs to move on into as yet uninhabited rooms.

Shadow

The early Carmelites established a lifestyle which would practically guarantee a confrontation with one's shadow. They encouraged quiet introspection through the prism of scripture; they gathered to point out the faults of the community members. Teresa of Avila's communities of friends were meant to undermine any claims to privilege based on bloodlines or virtue or anything else. Individuals were meant to be brought face-to-face with their essential poverty and learn to live in hope based on trust in God.

The shadow may be understood as the underside of the persona. When John of the Cross describes the beginner, the good religious person, in terms of the seven capital sins, he is identifying the shadow dimension of the religious persona. For example, the person is no longer obviously proud, but now has a secret pride in her growing humility and so forth.

What I am portraying to the world around, and what I believe about myself, has a dark side to it, an unacknowledged, unconscious aspect. The shadow is the inferior, undeveloped, negative aspect of the personality. It is a part of me I would not want others to know, nor do I want to know it myself. But prayer opens me to an inner journey into the truth of myself. That truth includes the shadow, and it is this reality that makes the inner journey initially painful. It is not simply a matter of acknowledging the fact that we have a shadow. Prayer may open us to the *expe-*

rience of the shadow. The challenge is to accept that this, too, is a part of who we are.

Teresa of Avila wrote about entering within herself and finding that she was at war with herself. John of the Cross talked about entering the misery of one's existence where all seemed to be operating in reverse, the opposite of what was assumed. The first Carmelites were warned that the devil, like a roaring lion, would stalk them in their inner desert. From a psychological point of view one could say that the authentic prayer of the mystics led them into an experience of the shadow side of their lives, the inferior, undeveloped, negative aspects of their personality. It certainly led them into an awareness of their sinfulness as well.

Prayer also led them into their giftedness and called them to accountability. This unknown dimension of the personality has been called the "positive" shadow. It, too needs, acceptance, and is often as painful to acknowledge and engage as are the more negative aspects of the shadow.

The mystics are particularly apt religious educators for adults. Generally, they are reporting experiences and convictions occurring in their mature years. Their stress on learning to listen attentively, to let go of tight control, to surrender to the Mystery addressing them from deep within their lives is advice given to adults who often have been struggling for years to find a path to greater meaning and life.

The sometimes strong ascetical language of entering into a dying process must be heard within the context of an adult life which is already gasping for air. The background to the message of the Carmelites is a day of normal human development before any talk of night. The Carmelites are addressing people who have some ego-strength with a persona in place, and who are in possession of a hard-won identity, world-view, and value system. These are the normal results of the first part of life. But it is a one-sided journey often leading to petrifaction. The person becomes restless, yearning for a saner, deeper, more fulfilling life, but nothing and no one is able to provide it.

It is into this situation of stagnation and dying that the message of letting go, surrendering in trust, is uttered. The message is not really bad news about jettisoning one's life, but good news about finding a way out of a situation of death. The accumulated wisdom of the Carmelites, which is simply a learning of gospel truths, is that the paschal mystery, the dying and rising of Christ, is built into human development. One need not go looking for crosses. To simply grow into the potential of one's life brings on death and its promise of resurrection.

Masculine and Feminine

The Carmelite tradition is a striking treasury of masculine and feminine imagery. These images speak to our yearning for both human community and also psychological wholeness. Masculine and feminine may be understood to refer not only to men and women, but also to modes of consciousness within each man and woman. Unless one is willing to separate sexuality from gender, it makes sense to say that the differences between males and females carry through into their personality structures. We have different, but related, inheritances. A healthy tradition will have to, in some way, assist an individual pilgrim to integrate the great polarity of human development signified by the symbols of masculine and feminine.

The far regions of the psyche are so different from the conscious personality that only a symbol of "otherness" can begin to express them. For men and women someone of the opposite sex is often the best expression of "otherness." Relating to that person, or to equivalent symbolic expressions, puts one in touch with nourishing sources of inner life. A healthy tradition makes available symbols of otherness, encouraging encounters which allow for a deeper, fuller life.

Very early in the history of Carmel, devotion to Mary found its way into the wadi. A medieval notion of the "lady of the place" may have made it natural for these rough hermits to dedicate the early chapel to Mary. The order continued throughout its history to place special emphasis on this woman, identifying itself as her brothers and calling her the "beauty of Carmel." The scapular worn by the men became special protective clothing given by

Mary. The order's relationship with Mary was such that it quickly became known as a Marian order and an advocate of Marian feasts and devotion.

The pair of Elijah and Mary are brought together most powerfully in *The Institution of the First Monks*. Each becomes the first of their gender to vow virginity, modeling for the Carmelite an expectancy of fulfillment. Not complete in themselves they await God's invitation to a relationship. For Carmelites they take on different gender roles, including "father" Elijah and "mother" Mary. This pair grows in stature in order legend and eventually they are understood by Arnold Bostius as co-founders.

Teresa of Avila and John of the Cross are names forever linked in the history of spirituality. The popular view of their relationship may assume a warmer friendship than was actually present. But as icons for the Carmelites they, together, form a masculine/feminine door through which the transcendent is approached. Carmelites are attracted to one or the other, not necessarily based on gender, but finding in John or Teresa a soul-mate. As Teresa advised, if you want to know God, know God's friends.

The whole ethos of the Teresian reform is formed by a web of relationships. It is impossible to think about the beginnings of the reform and not have in mind Teresa's numerous relationships with spiritual directors, theologians, missionaries, and assorted Carmelite friars. Her deep affection for Jerome Gratián, a leader of the reform among the male Carmelites, was quite absorbing for a period of time in her life.[9] Her relationship with John of the Cross was mutually enriching. She gave guidance and encouragement to the Carmelite men who pioneered the reform.

John often visited and stayed with many of Teresa's communities of women, saying mass, hearing confessions, counseling, teaching. They learned from him, as they testified, but he responded to them as well, attempting to put into writing his understanding of the spiritual life. He wrote important works at the request of women in his life: *The Spiritual Canticle* commentary for Ana de Jesús, the "captain" of Teresa's prioresses; and *The Living Flame of Love*, both poem and commentary, for the laywoman Ana de Peñalosa.

If relationship is a primary route for coming in contact with unmet psychological life within us, then the Carmel shaped by Teresa, John, and the early pioneers would have been conducive to such developments. Teresa pointed to the relationships among the sisters, and with outsiders, as a vernacular text for them to read. In that text they would come to know whether or not they were serving God. She wanted her sisters to be capable of affective, non-possessive relationships guided by adult discernment. She believed that in their relationships God was loving God.

Masculine and feminine symbols intertwine in the writings of Teresa and John as they attempt to describe their relationship with the Mystery at the center of their lives. Both mystics tell the story of the human/divine relationship as a love story, using images of man and woman, and their deepening union into marriage. Teresa describes a king at the center of the castle beckoning the feminine soul. John tells of a masculine beloved luring the feminine soul into high mountain trysts. John finds the initial plot of his story in the *Canticle* in the Old Testament, a love story portraying the relationship between God and God's people.

It should be no surprise that we cannot always find our contemporary sensitivity to gender issues in the writings of these saints. Teresa's complaints about her feminine nature seem to be part conditioning and part strategy. But a reader is forced to find some way of reconciling her sometimes apologetic language with her frequent bold assertions and action. She was not unaware of the prejudice against women: "Since the world's judges are sons of Adam and all of them men, there is no virtue in women that they do not hold suspect."[10]

John's writing conveys a spirituality in which many readers, both men and women, identify strong feminine elements. His use of the powerful image of a night in which one waits expectantly speaks of a receptivity which is often associated with the feminine. For some people the association is unfortunate and a stereotype. But for many others, it is appropriate and evocative, although limited.

Today's follower of the path of Carmel may or may not find the personalities of Teresa and John inviting. These mystics' use of particular images and symbols may sometimes be a barrier as well. But the mystery of the self we seek to know is revealed most aptly in the clothing of masculine and feminine imagery as well as in real women and men. The God whom we seek to follow is personal and more than personal and comes more fully into focus when seen through the prism of masculinity, femininity, and their relationship.

A Carmelite Contribution

If only the men in the wadi on Mount Carmel had kept journals, telling us about their motivations for being on the mountain, their reactions to its primitive conditions, their hopes for their new community! Only the Rule, formulated by an outside observer, and possibly the *Rubrica Prima*, the first article of the extant 1281 constitutions which testifies to their descent from Elijah and Elisha, give us windows into their early self-understanding as a community. Otherwise, we observe them from a distance, through pilgrims' diaries which comment on the presence of hermits in the wadi. It is tempting to believe that Nicholas the Frenchman, the future general and author of *The Flaming Arrow*, at one time had been with them in the wadi. Nicholas gives a human face and personality to the otherwise anonymous first generation of Carmelites.

Very possibly the triumphs and travails of Elijah the prophet became, for them, the archetypal stories of their own lives. They identified with his zealous defense of God, gloried in his defeat of the prophets of Baal, sympathized with his flight from persecutors, perhaps even recognized in his lassitude and discouragement their own emotional troughs. In Elijah, on whose mountain they lived and around whose well they gathered, they found patterns common to their own humanity.

The refounding of the order in the sixteenth century presents a very different picture. Teresa of Avila and John of the Cross left a literary heritage both intensely personal yet universal in its potential appeal. The writings of John and Teresa are striking in their perceptive analyses of both spiritual and psychological realities. It should not be surprising to find psychology and spirituality addressed in their works. These two processes most pointedly intersect in questions of human interiority and the nature of the self. The saints' primary concern was the presence of God in life, and the soul's response to God's will. But they were also well aware that this relationship between the soul and God affected mental and emotional states.

In our language today, Teresa and John encouraged a self-appropriation while at the same time they testified that the true self comes into reality only in self-transcendence. Teresa's language for self-appropriation is self-knowledge, which she bemoaned was in short supply. John observed the effect of disordered desires on the psyche and described it in the terms of the faculty psychology of his day. This psyche is never ignored or bypassed in relationship with God; hopefully, it is healed and brought to healthier functioning.

It is a Carmelite conviction that when the personality is not centered on this transcendent source of life and identity, but is centered on some part of God's creation, the personality is dysfunctional. Human development becomes a death scene. A part of God's creation is asked to be ultimate; it cannot bear the responsibility and so it begins to die under the burden. The personality which has created this idol in following its unhealed desires, also begins to die. A lesser god means a lesser human. True healing only comes with the death of alien gods in the psyche and the emergence of the Nameless One. That transformation is beyond the powers of the psyche and requires graced assistance, God's love healing, freeing, and uniting lover and beloved. De-absolutizing idols and waiting in hope for God's further self-revelation remains the constant Carmelite vocation.

But we only know ourselves and grow into healthy psychological functioning when we are following a call met within these very psyches, yet coming from beyond. A flame lures us deeper into the night; a shepherd whistles gently to come; a stag appears to lead the way. The Carmelite mystics became convinced that they were being invited, even *pursued* into greater life. We understand today that God's spirit enables our human spirit not to turn in on itself but to follow a call to go out to the other and to the ultimate Other. God is met and the self is born on the same journey.

When false gods die, the world which formerly competed

with God no longer preoccupies the heart. The soul is free to relate to and love this creation because it is now, in John's description, an harmonious symphony expressing the attributes of God. God is graceful as a mountain, pleasant as a valley, wonderful as a strange island, forceful and peaceful as a river; God is delightful as a breeze, restful and quiet as the night at the time of rising dawn. And God is the music, the solitude, the supper. God is all of these things, and they all speak of God to the soul. The outcome of a spiritual discipline which frees the heart from its attachments and compulsions is an enjoyment of the world in a non-possessive manner.

Teresa and John's description of the journey to and with God anticipates contemporary understandings of human development. Their accounts of transformation provide a developmental spiritual topography which parallels developmental theories. Developmental psychologists chart human development through crises, passages, and seasons as the personality undergoes transformation. Spirituality understands that freedom and authentic personhood result from a process of conversion underlying these personality changes. From a Christian perspective developmental theories are exploring not simply personality transformation, but manifestations of what is, at root, a graced invitation to surrender a life in trust to God's empowering love and mercy. Psychological constructs may be understood as a charting of the paschal mystery, the dying and rising of Christ, inbuilt in human development.

It is probable that both Teresa and John would have been very comfortable with today's attention to human interiority. Ego-development, shadow material, gender issues, active imagination, dream work, would all probably be of great interest to them. After all, in large measure their writings traced the impact of God's love on our fragile humanity. But, they would have insisted that beneath the world of ego, below any personal or collective unconscious, different from the realm of the archetypes, or whatever psychological categories one would choose to use, we eventually have to come to a transcendent source of identity. We are not our own cause, nor do we fully know our own identity. We ultimately find ourselves named.

It is interesting to watch Teresa become more psychologically sophisticated as she founds more communities. One can only imagine the enthusiasm present in a fast-growing reform supported by cities and monarchy alike. Very intense and zealous personalities would have been drawn to such a movement. Its contemplative demands would have furthered the development of those who came with healthy religious sensibilities. On the other hand, the atmosphere of such communities could exacerbate conditions of personality imbalance. In *The Foundations* Teresa shows a growing concern for unhealthy psychological responses and inauthentic spirituality.[11]

Psychological wholeness and spiritual holiness are not linked inseparably, nor are they totally unrelated. Psychological readiness for a full and faithful response to God is always a relative matter. All psyches are limited and a life of faith is a gift unmerited by anyone. Thérèse of Lisieux's "little way" is based on that fundamental Christian premise. On the other hand, the Carmelite mystics testified that their experience of God transformed and healed their psychic structures. Desires warring within them were reoriented and put at the service of God's will in their life.

We go to God who is beyond name and image through a world filled with words and images. It is a natural process and one should follow nature. A spiritual journey which begins to ignore the normal forms of prayer, religious imagery, and sacramental ritual risks becoming too ephemeral, too removed from the stuff of life. Both Teresa and John encourage traditional forms of religion, but remind us that none of it should take God's place. John observed that where there is faith, any image suffices; where there is no faith, no image suffices.

These Spanish mystics draw our attention beyond our own practices, even communal ones, and place emphasis on God's activity in our life. They encourage the concomitant attitude of listening, an attentiveness to God's approach. They have a preference for simple and silent atmospheres, both in outer environments, but especially in inner environments.

In this love for quiet and solitude, one can hear the prescriptions of the Rule permeating the attitudes of Teresa and John.

Teresa acknowledges that obedience or charity will often demand engagement with others, but "...I always repeat that solitude is better, and even that we must desire it."[12] And John writes to the nuns at Beas, "Speaking distracts one, while silence and work recollects and strengthens the spirit."[13] It is also the preferred atmosphere of their sons and daughters, such as Lawrence of the Resurrection and Thérèse of Lisieux.

The first Carmelites must have wrestled with their personalities as they attempted to live in allegiance to Jesus Christ. Their lives were structured in such a way that they could not escape themselves, nor their devils, nor the God who was pursuing them. They knew that their salvation lay in such unremitting engagement.

Teresa of Avila and John of the Cross, paradigms of humanity, teach that authentic human development is ultimately a process of divinization, a participation in the knowing and loving of God. These mystics report a graciousness at the core of life, a transcendent source of identity and empowerment within the psyche, which nurtured and guaranteed their personhood.

NOTES

1. Cf. Appendix for Carmelite Rule

2. For a psychological discussion of Teresa's imagery cf. John Welch, *Spiritual Pilgrims: Carl Jung and Teresa of Avila* (New York: Paulist Press, 1982).

3. The person has a psychological structure composed of sensory and spiritual components. Each component has faculties, or powers, which have an appetite to be fulfilled. It was John's conviction that these faculties are expressive of a fundamental human hunger for which only God is sufficient food. Cf. John Welch, *When Gods Die: An Introduction to John of the Cross* (New York: Paulist Press, 1990).

4. "Everyone can call to mind friends or schoolmates who were promising and idealistic youngsters, but who, when we meet them again years later, seem to have grown dry and cramped in a narrow mould....

The nearer we approach to the middle of life, and the better we have succeeded in entrenching ourselves in our personal attitudes and social positions, the more it appears as if we had discovered the right course and the right ideals and principles of behaviour. For this reason we suppose them to be eternally valid, and make a virtue of unchangeably clinging to them. We overlook the essential fact that the social goal is attained only at the cost of a diminution of personality." C.G. Jung, *Collected Works* (Princeton University Press, 1969), VIII, pars. 770, 772.

5. "Among all my patients in the second half of life–that is to say, over thirty-five–there has not been one whose problem in the last resort was not that of finding a religious outlook on life. It is safe to say that every one of them fell ill because he had lost what the living religions of every age have given to their followers, and none of them has been really healed who did not regain his religious outlook." C.G. Jung, *Collected Works*, XI, par. 509.

Jung believed that alcoholic addiction expressed a spiritual hunger and could be counteracted through a spiritual renewal and the support of human community. Members of twelve-step programs often comment on the compatibility between their program and Carmelite spirituality.

6. Jung observed that there is a great difference between the person whose sun circles their earth and the person whose earth has learned to circle the sun.

7. For example, Teresa taught that prayer is never so lofty that meditation on the humanity of Christ becomes unnecessary: "They have contradicted me about it and said that I don't understand, because these are paths along which our Lord leads, and that when souls have already passed beyond the beginning stages it is better for them to deal with things concerning the divinity and flee from corporeal things. Nonetheless, they will not make me admit that such a road is a good one." Teresa of Avila, *The Interior Castle* in *The Collected Works of St. Teresa of Avila,* 2, trans. Kieran Kavanaugh, O.C.D., and Otilio Rodriguez, O.C.D. (Washington, D.C.: ICS Publications, 1980), The Sixth Dwelling Places, chap. 7, no. 5.

8. "Worst of it all is that intelligent and cultivated people live their lives without even knowing of the possibility of such transformations. Wholly unprepared, they embark upon the second half of life. Or are there perhaps colleges for forty-year-olds which prepare them for their coming life and its demands as the ordinary colleges introduce our young people to a knowledge of the world? No, thoroughly unprepared we take the step into the afternoon of life; worse still, we take this step with the false assumption that our truths and ideals will serve us as hitherto. But we cannot live the afternoon of life according to the programme of life's morning; for what was great in the morning will be little at evening, and what in the morning was true will at evening have become a lie." C.G. Jung, *The Collected Works*, VIII, par. 784.

9. Jerónimo Gratián was already ordained when he entered the Carmelite novitiate in 1572. He became a dedicated religious and gifted administrator. Teresa considered him a blessing from God for the reform, as well as for her personally. After Teresa's death, disagreements within the reform led to Gratián's expulsion.

10. Teresa of Avila, *The Way of Perfection*, in *The Collected Works,* 2, chap. 3, no. 7.

11. "I know some souls of great virtue who remained for seven or eight hours in absorption....I find no benefit in this bodily weakness–for it is nothing else–except that it arises from a good source, It would be a greater help to use this time well than to remain in this absorption so long. Much more can be merited by making an act of love and by often awakening the will to greater love of God than by leaving it listless. So I counsel the prioresses to make every possible effort to prevent the nuns from spending long periods in this daze." Teresa of Avila, *The Foundations* in *The Collected Works*, 3, chap. 6, nos. 2 and 5.

12. Teresa of Avila, *The Foundations,* in *The Collected Works*, 3, chap 5, no. 15.

13. John of the Cross, *The Letters,* in *The Collected Works of St. John of the Cross,* trans. Kieran Kavanaugh, O.C.D., and Otilio Rodriguez, O.C.D. (Washington, D.C.: ICS Publications, 1991), 741.

Chapter Seven

MEN, WOMEN, AND CONTEMPLATION

Gender Issues in the Spiritual Life

It is tempting to say the Carmelite Order was begun by a group of "wild men" gathered in a wadi on a mountainous ridge jutting out into the Mediterranean. It is hard to imagine a more primitive setting, and it is certainly one that would warm the heart of anyone today seeking to recover the masculine. The mountain constellated myths about it, particularly the stories of that original "wild man," Elijah the Tishbite.

These men embraced the feminine quickly, but welcoming actual women took a little longer. They identified themselves as brothers of the Virgin Mary and named their chapel in her honor. In their sensitivity to the feminine and honoring "the lady of the place" these spiritual warriors were true to their medieval heritage.

But they were not as quick to accept women into the order. Unlike other mendicant groups which developed both men and women's communities, the Carmelites successfully fended off responsibility for a women's branch for over two hundred years. Almost from the beginning some women were affiliated with local communities, but these were individual cases. John Soreth, a fifteenth-century general of the order, established the first communities of Carmelite women. Today, especially because of the impact made on the church and the wider society by the Teresian communities of women, large segments of the church are unaware of the existence of Carmelite men.

Anonymity of Carmelite men is, perhaps, a minor issue, but it calls to mind the paucity of attention given to the situation of men in the church today. Without denying the need to further explore the role of women in society and church, some additional thought needs to be given to the complicated situation of men. Undoubtedly the feminine has blessings to bestow upon humankind, but what is the masculine contribution today?

This chapter explores the psychological journeys of women and men. It is an attempt to name some of the characteristics or issues which may be particular to one or the other gender. If there are such gender-related characteristics, they should emerge as prayer leads one into the reality of the self.

While both feminine and masculine psychology are discussed, the greater part of this chapter is devoted to theories regarding the man's development. With the emphasis on the feminine today, men are searching for a deeper understanding of their own masculinity. However, whenever talking about one or the other gender, often the characteristics are recognized as common to both. Hopefully, a discussion of the masculine will also be beneficial to women, perhaps in understanding themselves, but also in better understanding men.

Vasalisa's Doll

In a class on spirituality and human development at the Washington Theological Union, we were studying feminine and masculine psychology and spirituality. For women's psychology we read a story from Clarissa Pinkola Estés' book, *Women Who Run with the Wolves*.[1] Two of the women in class summarized the material, presented their reactions to it and led the discussions. The story we discussed from Estés' book was about a young girl named Vasalisa.

Vasalisa is given a doll by her dying mother. After the mother's death, the doll becomes a sure guide for the young girl. The father remarries and Vasalisa now has a stepmother and stepsisters. Her new family does not like the girl. They want to get rid of her, so they tell her that the flame in the house has gone out and that she will have to go into the woods to Baba Yaga's house to fetch a new fire. They hope she will never return.

Naturally, there are dangers on the journey, but the doll in her pocket keeps giving her good advice. She safely arrives at Baba Yaga's house. Estés describes Baba Yaga:

> Now the Baba Yaga was a very fearsome creature. She traveled, not in a chariot, not in a coach, but in a cauldron shaped like a mortar which flew along all by itself. She rowed this vehicle with an oar shaped like a pestle, and all the while she swept out the tracks of where she'd been with a broom made of long-dead persons' hair.
>
> And the cauldron flew through the sky with Baba Yaga's own greasy hair flying behind. Her long chin curved up and her long nose curved down, and they met in the middle. She had a tiny white goatee and warts on her skin from her trade in toads. Her brown-stained fingernails were thick and ridged like roofs, and so curled over she could not make a fist.
>
> Even more strange was the Baba Yaga's house. It sat atop huge, scaly yellow chicken legs, and walked about all by itself and sometimes twirled around and around like an ecstatic dancer. The bolts on the doors and shutters were made of human fingers and toes and the lock on the front door was a snout with many pointed teeth.[2]

Vasalisa bravely asks for fire. Baba Yaga replies that she first must perform many tasks before getting the fire. The tasks turn out to be impossible, but the doll in Vasalisa's pocket accomplishes the tasks for her.

Baba Yaga finally gives her the flame. It is in a skull and it shines out the eyes. Vasalisa returns home with the fiery skull, and the flame streaming from its eyes burns the stepmother and stepsisters to cinders.

An Interpretation

Estés interprets the story of Vasalisa as a story about a woman finding her true feminine nature. The doll given her by her mother is her matrilineal heritage which can be a true guide. The frightening hag, Baba Yaga, is an image of the woman's instinctual self, her primal core. In Baba Yaga's house Vasalisa gets in tune with her true nature, finds her own voice, and is able to return with her own fire. With that wisdom she is able to detect and defeat inauthentic, controlling voices around her, as well as the ones she has internalized.

Estés stories continually amplify her theme that woman must find the wild woman inside. Drawing on her hispanic heritage she calls this deep layer of identity the *rio abajo del rio* (the river below the river), or the *canto hondo* (the deep song).

The young girl has several developmental tasks before receiving the fire: letting the too-good mother die, both outside of her and inside her; coming to know her own shadow side as she lets go of the overly positive mother; learning to trust and follow and feed her intuition; facing the Wild Hag, Baba Yaga, her inner feminine nature without wavering (Estés comments that not only men are afraid of women's power!); serving the non-rational, acclimating herself to the "great wildish powers of the feminine psyche"; separating this from that, learning to make fine distinctions in judgment; eventually taking on new, immense power to see and affect others, looking at her life situations in a new light.

It is Estés' conviction that women have a soul-hunger. She encourages recovering the "wild woman." The name evokes the archetypal, the intuitive, the sexual and cyclical, the ages of women, a woman's way, a woman's knowing, her creative fire. To quote Estés, this wild woman has become "ghostly from neglect, buried by over-domestication, outlawed by surrounding culture, no longer understood anymore."[3]

Estés analysis is that when a woman is cut away from her basic source, when her instincts and natural life cycles are lost, subsumed by the culture, or by the intellect or the ego–one's own or those belonging to others–then it is time to recover the innate spiritual being at the center of feminine psychology.

Estés points to fleeting tastes of the wild; they come through beauty as well as loss: during pregnancy, while nursing a child, during the change in oneself in raising a child, during a love relationship tended like a garden. They come while seeing sights of great beauty, sunsets, fishermen coming up from the lake at dusk with lanterns lit. They come in the sound of music which vibrates the sternum, excites the heart—the drum, the whistle, the call. All may be tastes of the wild and reminds us that "one has given scant time to the mystic cookfire or to the dreamtime, too little time to one's own creative life, one's life work, or one's true loves."[4]

Men, the Problem

In listening to talks and reading texts in the areas of spirituality and theology, a man cannot help but be slightly overwhelmed by the emphasis on the feminine in church discourse today, often with an accompanying critique of the masculine. In many discussions, masculine domination is viewed as the culprit—control of the church, control of theological sources, control or domination of dialogue within the church.

Men, too, see many of the problems. We see the overwhelmingly masculine leadership in the church. We realize theology may be used inappropriately to prop up such structures. We, too, are embarrassed about the weight given to non-issues such as altar girls.

We see many of the problems, but we hear in many spoken and unspoken ways that *men are the problem*! Often discussion seems to imply that men, by their nature, just by being men, are responsible for many of today's problems.

I remember a discussion I had with two women religious who were quite upset with the masculine church. I said, while I realize that most of the positions of authority in the church are held by men, as a man I experience the church as quite feminine. The two women could not imagine how I could say the church seems quite feminine.

Women are often the chief nurturers of a young boy's faith. Women, certainly in the past, strongly encouraged a young man to enter church ministry. But if it is necessary for a young man to pull away from home and family in order to find his own identity and adulthood, entering ordained ministry, at least at an early age, may be experienced as simply an extension of the control of homelife. The boy has moved from his own mother to Mother Church without a pause in between to find himself. He goes from one situation where he was being named by others and told how to behave, to another more powerful situation where he is again named by others and shaped in his behaviors.

The young man may have had to fight as hard for his identity in the church as he did at home. The persona of priesthood is quite strong, and keeping in touch with oneself within that persona may be difficult. The experience of the church for a man can be one of a controlling, smothering, womb-like existence.

With all the talk of the dominance of the masculine and the problems men generate, one would think the last thing the world needs is more masculine, let alone more wild men. But some authors today say there is not enough of the right kind of masculine. They write about another, more mature masculine that needs to be attended to.

In this analysis, men too have trouble finding *their* inner voice, their innate masculinity. Some of the blame is placed on the patriarchy itself, that form of the masculine often associated with control, power, domination, manipulation, competition, aggressiveness, abuse, and so forth. If this is the only kind of masculinity offered a man, then patriarchy is not only an attack on the feminine but it also is an attack on the truly masculine. The structures and dynamics of patriarchy can trap a man in his fears of both women and other men.

Part of the blame is placed on absent fathers, physically or emotionally absent. No one is available to mentor the young man into other dimensions of the masculine.

Some of the blame is also placed on the lack of rituals which could initiate a man into a responsible adulthood. Victor Turner observed we no longer have rituals, but "mere ceremonials." They do not have real power to achieve genuine transformation.

The result of a confining patriarchy, the lack of caring father figures, and the absence of transforming rituals is a type of masculine that certain authors call "boy psychology." Robert Moore and Douglas Gillette in their book on masculine psychology, *King, Warrior, Magician, Lover*, argue the marks of boy psychology are easy to see around us:

> ...abusive and violent acting-out behaviors against others, both men and women; passivity and weakness, the inability to act effectively and creatively in one's own life and to engender life and creativity in others (both men and women); and, often, an oscillation between the two—abuse/weakness, abuse/weakness.[5]

Boy Psychology

As a boy grows up there are several stages of development leading to adolescence, all of them belonging to what could be called the immature masculine, or boy psychology. The presence of loving adults greatly helps the boy's development: he develops a basic trust in himself and in life; a secure and competent ego emerges; he adjusts to society's norms and values.

What damages a boy's development is a lack of response to his attachment needs, or the use of threats of abandonment, or inducing guilt in the boy, or parental clinging to the child. Potentially, the most disastrous occurrence for a developing child is the loss of parents or the loss of caring adults.

From the first efforts to play with toys, and crawl in exploration of the world, the boy is finding transitional objects and behaviors which will assist him in moving away from the parents and into his own identity and adult life. It is the archetypal journey of the hero.

Joseph Campbell identified stages of the hero's quest. The hero receives a call to adventure and sets out from his home. After he has crossed some kind of threshold he is subjected to a series of trials and ordeals. Eventually, he undergoes the supreme ordeal, which is the fight with the monster. When, finally, he defeats the monster, he is rewarded with the treasure hard to attain, that is, the throne of the kingdom and the beautiful princess as his bride.

In adolescence the boy/hero has certain developmental tasks: a loosening of the bonds to the parents (who no longer shimmer as gods), a sense of identity, confidence as an adult member of one's sex, a competent social role, sexual maturity, a readiness to marry and so forth. While the young girl has similar tasks there is some thought that a boy may have to make a more radical break from parents, especially the mother, in order to find his identity.

Because spiritual writers in the Carmelite tradition are adults addressing adults, their message may need careful interpretation for a young person in this first part of life. Certainly, without interpretation, their warnings to avoid attachments could be interpreted as a warning against any involvement in life at all. They could be interpreted as advising avoidance of commitments, responsibilities, relationships, care for this world. They could be understood as saying that the young person will have a more direct route to God if he or she can avoid life's entanglements.

To the young person, the mystics' call for detachment is not an excuse for avoiding life but an encouragement to leave the womb of the unconscious, to fight the inertia of collectivity, to step forward into one's life and become someone. The liberation called for in the first half of life is a freedom from the enslavement of the dark forces which undermine personhood and stifle the development of values and competency. Psychologically, sin is a refusal to come to consciousness, wrote Carl Jung. A contemplative stance at this time in life should assist one in hearing more clearly and responding to the archetypal forces which come online within the personality. And an important early archetypal story telling itself within the individual and moving him or her more fully into a unique life, is the story of the hero.

In reality, the Carmelite mystics are addressing men and women who have entered into life fully, have been committed to it, are passionate about it, and who find themselves fragmented and still hungering for a fulfillment which continually escapes them. At this point in life the mystics' call for detachment, liberation of the heart, is not a call to disengage but to let die what has taken God's place and is now a source of death, not life. It is a call to hear within the debris of one's life the offer of a love which has not disappeared and will not disappoint.

Man Psychology

The analysis of some writers is that the hero story is about this transition from adolescence to adulthood, not about the man's growth into a deeper masculinity. The hero story represents the culmination of boy psychology. The reason we never hear about the hero and the princess after he wins her is that he does not know what to do with her.

These authors argue that further development, development beyond the hero's adventure, is required so that a man may attain a more mature masculine. This "man psychology" as distinct from a "boy psychology," is not attained through greater integration of the feminine, as important as that may be. At this point what is needed is less feminine. Men often feel overwhelmed by the feminine. What is needed is more masculine, a masculine connected to the deep and instinctual masculine energies, the potentials of the mature masculine.

Although our culture no longer provides rites of initiation, there persists in all of us, regardless of gender, an archetypal need to be initiated. Attainment of a new stage of life, a more mature masculine, for example, seems to demand that symbols of initiation, appropriate to that stage, must be experienced. The masculine principle, in particular, seems to demand culturally sanctioned trials and ordeals if it is to achieve full actualization in maturity. Therapists report that there is an *initiation hunger* in many people going into analysis. If society fails to provide a suitable initiation, then there must be a self-initiation. The man must enter into a deeper relationship with himself, become an authority in the nuances of his own experience, define manhood for himself.

Sam Keen in *Fire in the Belly*[6] identifies two stages in the development of a more mature masculine. The first stage of the journey, The Soulful Quest, is a pilgrimage into the depths of the self. Homecoming, the second stage, is a return to the everyday world with a new sense of self, new virtues and a new understanding of virility. It may be understood as the journey of the hero once more, but into neglected regions of the masculine psyche.

It is not a stretch to say that this process is best done contemplatively, with a listening attitude and a faith that one is being addressed in the depths of one's being by a transcendent source of identity. So used to wording his reality, a man is asked to listen and endure what he hears. It is a listening to one's depths, a psychological task but also a religious pilgrimage. The self-knowledge encouraged by Teresa of Avila, for example, certainly includes psychological discovery where appropriate, but such knowledge is more fruitfully gained in an encounter with the Mystery met within the psyche yet from beyond it. If the psychological experiences and insights become more interesting and absorbing than the transcendent source of identity, then one is heading back out the door of the castle.

The beginning of such a journey that is both psychological and spiritual is usually not the result of an unpressured decision. Often, something invites our attention. For example, Clarissa Pinkola Estés, in talking about the woman's point of departure, identifies many things which may be a door opening to this process. She says if you have a deep scar, that is the door to begin the journey; if you have an old, old story, that is a door; if you love the sky and the water so much you almost cannot bear it, that is a door; if you yearn for a deeper life, a full life, a sane life, that is a door. Remember Teresa writing, "I wanted to live...but I had no one to give me life...."

Sam Keen says it can begin with the death of a parent, a spouse, a friend. It may happen through boredom and the urge to run away. Perhaps it begins when we are overwhelmed by the plight of the world's starving and poor; when we age and feel vulnerable. He writes: "Call it midlife crisis, depression, alienation, the dark night of the soul, the opening of a new path. Honor it. Listen. Respond....Good-by to the stereotyped roles—of rich man poor man, doctor, lawyer, merchant, chief—of warrior and conquistador."[7]

John of the Cross says it may begin when you find your normal thought processes are not able to sort out your world. When John identifies an inability to meditate, he is saying we can no longer word our life as before. The normal strategies are not working. And this sense of powerlessness is probably not helped by being thrown into prison by one's brothers in religion. Being mute within and voiceless without must certainly plunge one into an intense silence.

Teresa might say it happens when your carefully controlled life starts to come apart. Your tidy rooms in the castle are no longer enough. She identifies times when God can break through even a good, virtuous life.

A dying process is beginning. Something is being sloughed off. For any new life to happen, old life has to give way. Clarissa Estés speaks about letting the too-good mother die. There is much more to the woman than she has been allowed thus far to claim. Jung wrote about the woman carrying man's feminine dimension for him, thereby excusing him from knowing himself more deeply, and keeping the woman from finding her own feminine reality. Sebastian Moore refers to this situation as, "Seeing your life through somebody else's eyes."

In speaking about men, Sam Keen argues, at some point "we must kick dad and mother, priest, pope and president out of our psyche and seize the authority for our own lives. We must become responsible for our own values and visions....Growing into the fullness of our humanity means that we become co-authors of the rules by which we will agree to have our lives judged."[8]

The contemplative would argue that this process happens most authentically when the personality is reoriented around a center which is experienced as Otherness. From this center comes a new identity. A man is learning to shift from a stance of being his own ground to trusting an unknown Ground. As John of the Cross writes, a man has to take off his shoes and walk reverently because his journey is on sacred ground. He does not know the way, nor does he have the provisions. He is learning to be led and fed.

The mystics warn that this contemplative journey, this "loving attentiveness," can be quite difficult and confusing along the way, especially initially, as hard-earned identities are set aside and a person begins to walk a less clear, less sure path. It may be so disconcerting that John was able to write: "Everything seems to be functioning in reverse."

John of the Cross describes this night as a loving experience of God. Nothing in the love is confusing, dark, or painful, but it is because of who we are that this love initially darkens us. Before, we knew by knowing; now, we know by an unknowing. It is poverty of spirit; it is contemplation, an openness to God's transforming love as it approaches us in a dark way.

A psychological agenda may surface in this contemplative process. Keen describes what it might mean for a man:

> We leave the sunlit world of easy roles and prefabricated tokens of masculinity, penetrate the character armor, get beneath the personality, and plunge into the chaos and pain of the old "masculine" self. This isn't the fun part of the trip. It's spelunking in Plato's cave, feeling our way through the illusions we have mistaken for reality, crawling through the drain sewers where the forbidden "unmanly" feelings dwell, confronting the demons and dark shadows that have held us captive from their underground haunts. In this stage of the journey we must make use of the warrior's fierceness, courage, and aggression to break through the rigidities of old structures of manhood, and explore the dark and taboo "negative" emotions that make up the shadow of modern manhood.[9]

John of the Cross encourages entering the dark of the experience with patience and trust, and perseverance. It is a time for going quiet, a time for listening, for being a "watch in the night." There are different ways of describing what is going on: a crucifixion, losing ego, descending into hell, battling dragons, encountering demons. Keen warns that we lose a spiritual dimension to this experience if we simply name it stress, depression, or burnout. It may be difficult for a man to believe that anything of value is happening unless he is in control. To man's impatience, John of the Cross says, be patient.

To man's deep mistrust of the universe, John says enter this dark time with trust. A graciousness is at work which will not fail us.

Homecoming

But there does come a turning point. Somehow, where there apparently had been death, life is reborn. Keen comments that the experience is like a traveler laying a burden down, a falsely accused man recovering his innocence, the prodigal son returning home, a bone slipping back into its socket. John of the Cross writes about the night that slowly becomes a guide, a flame which begins to heal, an absence which gives way to Presence. The path of the soulful quest begins to turn upward.

Keen tries to identify times when this graciousness becomes apparent:

> Such moments of grace may overtake you while you are dancing, eating cold cereal, watching a commercial on TV, making love, sitting still and thinking about nothing in particular. It happened to Martin Luther when he was sitting on the toilet. After years of being constipated and compulsive it occurred to him that his life was of ultimate worth not because of any work he accomplished, but because he was accepted by God even as he remained a constipated sinner. No sooner did it occur to him that "I live by the grace of God," than his bowels opened, his anal compulsive personality underwent a conversion, and the Protestant Reformation began.[10]

While the Christian has a goal of self-forgetfulness, it cannot be done until we have a self-remembrance. Until we remember ourselves, we remain a problem to ourselves. We can be self-absorbed, compulsively introspective, and narcissistic. We do not really have self-love. It is when we are able to grow into a deep sense of self-acceptance that we can forget the self.

What will a man look like today as he emerges from a heroic journey in which he has had to jettison old identities confront his shadow, face hidden fears, and renew links with life forces deep within him?

As I read about the potential for a renewal or recovery of a different kind of masculine, I kept thinking about two characters I have been following in several historical novels written by Patrick O'Brian. O'Brian has created a remarkable series of stories involving a British naval captain during the Napoleonic Wars and his friend who is the ship's surgeon. Some aspects of the new masculine, it seems to me, may involve a combination of qualities exemplified in these two figures.

Jack Aubrey, the British naval officer, is an old-fashioned hero. He strides the quarterdeck of his sailing vessels in complete command. His ships are usually not the best nor largest in the fleet, but his crews are well trained and dedicated, and Aubrey overcomes the odds by his uncommon navigational ability and meticulous preparation. His loyalties are to the British Crown and the naval service. He is fearless and fierce in battle, compassionate in victory. Life on his ships reaches a dramatic high point on Sundays when the ship is rigged for church. The men are arranged according to ship's divisions, Episcopal prayer services are followed, and Jack Aubrey reads the Articles of War. His men generally appreciate this orderly and disciplined world. Almost every evening they are called to general quarters and practice firing the great guns with speed and accuracy.

Steven Maturin, his long-time friend, is usually the ship's surgeon on Aubrey's voyages. Maturin lives below decks, working to heal those who have become ill during the long voyages or wounded in intense battles. His loyalties are not to the Crown. He is Irish and Papist and part of his youth was spent living in Spain. He does not have a thirst for action, but as a naturalist he appreciates the opportunity to visit strange lands and observe new species. He often reports back to scientific societies. Frequently, however, he suffers disappointments as the ship sails past a particularly promising island. His friend Aubrey has orders to follow and a mission to accomplish, and, as usual, "there is not a moment to lose!"

The two men are quite dissimilar. The tall, imposing Aubrey went to sea at an early age and, consequently, his education focused on sciences which allowed for accurate navigation and all that goes into commanding a man of war. He speaks only English. On land he is out of his element. Marriage, family, property, investments are welcome and respected realities but he is awkward around them. He is truly comfortable only when land is fading astern, sails are beginning to billow, deep waters beckon, and a regular routine of life at sea commences.

The short, nondescript Maturin is broadly educated and a polyglot, often speaking in Latin when he wants to consult with another medical man in privacy. He is clumsy at sea, usually falling between ships when transferring from one to another. His clothing is generally an afterthought, his wig unkempt and crooked. He pretends interest in his friend's explanations of ship matters and battle sequences, just as Aubrey feigns interest when Stephen begins to describe a rare species, or becomes enthusiastic about something discovered while dissecting a specimen. They gladly put up with one another's passionate interests because of their friendship.

Jack Aubrey and Stephen Maturin appreciate, and perhaps call forth, the best in one another. And when one is not his best, the other stands as a reminder of forgotten virtue. Their friendship, as a whole, forms a collage of masculine qualities. The strengths of each man tend toward an extreme but are tempered by the other. Would a mature masculine be, in some way, a composite of such men?

Sam Keen believes the new heroic man will not look like the traditional hero; perhaps he will look the opposite of a traditional hero. He perhaps will have more modesty and humility. He may not be as visible because he has given up the conceit that any man is "larger than life." He will be marked by a new willingness to fit in, to be a part of the whole. He will not need the spotlight as much. His life may have great dignity but lack the kind of dramatic largeness of the traditional hero. Keen names some of the virtues or characteristics which may be part of the new hero:

Wonder

The new hero will pause to wonder and to see the world as wonderful. Through contemplation, John of the Cross describes the world becoming a symphony. Without wonder, men remain compulsively active, perhaps becoming experts and efficient professionals, but also possibly becoming puppets and functionaries of institutions. Wonder opens up greater possibilities in life.

Stephen Maturin becomes absorbed in watching a school of dolphins playfully accompanying the ship. The seas grow rougher, the waves higher, the troughs deeper. Suddenly, as the ship descends deeply into a trough, the dolphins rise in a wave and appear before Stephen; he is looking directly at them through a translucent wall of water. Then the moment passes; the ship rises, the dolphins subside with the water.

Empathy

The new hero, after remembering himself, now can forget himself and be available to others. He is an "available" person. He flows out to others with a natural empathy. Keen observes: "Empathic men have stepped out of the hierarchical way of viewing relationships where you are either one up or one down, and have become cobeings."[11] My father never liked to talk about someone working for him; they always worked *with* him.

Men with this empathic virtue do not talk at people, they do not interrupt, they do not give advice. They listen and stand beside you, and in their presence you have the feeling that you are allowed, even encouraged, to be yourself.

After sorting through observations about men's behavior, perhaps the most pointed, practical advice one could give men is to *listen*, especially to women. By listening, men learn what they have been missing, and by being listened to, women are helped to find their voice. Such advice may seem patronizing to both men and women, but it is worth the risk.

Heartfelt Mind

Howard Thurman, formerly dean of the chapel at Howard Divinity school in Washington, D.C., talked about listening to the rhythm of one's own time, life, body. He advised learning to "simmer" in the morning and evening. Apparently he meant to take time to know not only what I truly think, but also how life is affecting me at depth. A heartfelt mind seems best done by cultivating a discipline of solitude, and the habit of recollection and autobiographical thinking.

Both Aubrey and Maturin, alone in their respective cabins, in long letters to their wives, written over thousands of miles of sailing, sort through their actions and motives. The letters may never reach their wives; they may never actually be sent. But in these lines the two men sort through their moods, and word what is often only dimly perceived. They take their own pulse, as well as the pulse of the ship. In this activity they catch up with themselves, bring themselves up to date, and find their bearings.

Moral Outrage

Writers affirm the need to maintain a warrior dimension in men. These contemporary warriors are men who are alive with moral outrage and who are willing to wrestle with the mystery of evil in one of its many disguises. They become warriors in defense of the sacred–not able to save every single suffering, child, but reducing the *number* of suffering children. The contemplative tradition is actually the deepest source of compassion for the world. It is not inimical to social justice concerns.

Besides being the ship's surgeon, and a naturalist, and a man who is decidedly non-military, Stephen Maturin is also an intelligence agent for Britain. While Jack Aubrey pursues the tasks his orders demand of him, Maturin often has his own secret orders which involve coded messages and clandestine meetings. Aubrey is only slightly aware of the intelligence activities of his friend, but out of respect for their friendship he asks no questions. He supports Stephen's endeavors as best he can. Stephen undertakes these missions not out of loyalty to Britain, but out of determined opposition to Bonaparte and in support of Catalan independence.

When ashore and carrying out a secret mission Stephen is as

determined as Jack Aubrey is in a naval engagement. Shipmates who see Stephen coming down a street in the seaport are mistaken when they assume they know him well, throw their arms about him, and invite him to come with them for a drink. Stephen shrugs off their gestures, and passes through their midst with a fierce look in his eye.

Right Livelihood

What to do in life? Joseph Campbell says, "Follow your bliss!" Keen asks: What are your gifts? What gives you the greatest joy? What have you to offer?

Many people, perhaps most, have an occupation that differs from their vocation. We may find such a situation tolerable if our occupation does not do violence to our vocation. But it is crucial to find a way to incarnate our care. It is equally important to look for the transcendent in our ordinary life of work.

Enjoyment

The one spiritual disease of men Keen would identify above others is the *lack of joy*. He maintains that a cure lies in reviving atrophying senses: bird-watching, walking, visiting, working a garden, playing ball in the streets, playing music, reading, doing nothing.

After the sails have been trimmed for night sailing, the watch has been set, and the ship settles down for the night, Aubrey and Maturin will sometimes sit down in the Captain's cabin with their violin and cello and follow one another through their favorite classical music. The sound leaks though the timbers and carries out over the dark waters.

Friendship

Friendship with other men offers a type of validation and acceptance that can only be received from someone of the same gender. Such friendships may help counter the alienation which often occurs in corporate and professional styles of life.

The core of Patrick O'Brian's stories of the sea is the friendship between two men. Fortunes wax and wane, battles are won and lost, relationships with others fray and heal; but there is a constancy in their affection and appreciation for one another. No matter how stormy the night or difficult the situation, no matter how tired or out of sorts, they are always genuinely pleased to see one another and their greetings and observations are gentle, respectful, and heartfelt. When a sharp or impatient word does occur between them it is almost a shock to the reader.

Community/Communion

We have ignored the fundamental truth of interdependence, the inescapable call to community. Twelve-step groups have reestablished that truth. The second part of the heroic journey, Homecoming, takes place within the bonds of community.

The Carmelite mystics emphasized that the quality of one's community life was an indication of the authenticity of one's prayer. Through his contemplative prayer, John of the Cross learned to esteem his sisters and brothers and not judge them. Such a result leads to the conclusion that true community is formed from the relationship each has, not only with the others, but with God at the center of the community.

Husbanding

A husbandman takes care of the place with which he has been entrusted. Psychologically, the husbandman is a one who makes commitments, puts down roots, and incarnates his compassion and empathy in actions of caring. He may have been on the road a long time, but he now has the courage to come home again and tend a single spot with the wisdom gained during his pilgrimage.

Wildness

Here Keen returns to the idea that both men and women may be over-domesticated and kept from being in touch with the life-giving forces at the core of their identity.

I imagine that the church's acceptance of an order's original charisms, and the order's gradual institutionalization, would tend to domesticate the men and women attempting to live that tradition. Does the contemplative impulse within the tradition provide a means for recovering our "wildish" powers? If contemplation means the openness to God's transforming love, no matter how it is approaching us, then it makes some sense that the new life within us will have gender related characteristics.

For twenty years Keen has been giving workshops helping men identify their personal myths. When he asks them to draw their ideal living environment, almost all draw an isolated setting near a lake, a sea or in mountains or a desert. It reminds one of the "wild men" on Mount Carmel!

NOTES

1. Clarissa Pinkola Estés, *Women Who Run with the Wolves* (New York: Ballantine Books, 1992), 75–80.

2. Ibid., 77.

3. Ibid., 7.

4. Ibid.

5. Robert Moore and Douglas Gillette, *King, Warrior, Magician, Lover* (HarperSanFrancisco, 1990), xvi.

6. Sam Keen, *Fire in the Belly* (New York: Bantam Books, 1991).

7. Ibid., 130.

8. Ibid., 144, 145.

9. Ibid., 127, 128.

10. Ibid., 150.

11. Ibid., 157.

Chapter Eight

VISIONS AND VOICES
Extraordinary Religious Experiences

Our age appears, at times, to be quite schizophrenic. Sometimes it appears that we believe in nothing; at other times, it seems we will believe in anything. Our hunger for something spiritual, something which transcends our everyday world, leaves us open to the strangest of claims. We see and hear things that, to say the least, are unusual.

On the border between psyche and spirit lie the strange occurrences of visions and voices. In the past, extraordinary experiences were closely identified with the mystics. Mystics were those Christians who had unusual experiences which were not naturally possible. Mystics were people who levitated, bilocated, flew, spoke to the dead, saw the future and in general heard and saw things the rest of us could not hear or see.

Because of the interest in such unusual happenings it was difficult to hear the much more down-to-earth teachings of the mystics about the ordinary Christian life of faith. It is more interesting for us to speculate on the meanings of prophecies, to wonder about secrets supposedly given to so and so, to look for the sun that dances, the statue that weeps, the rosary that turns to gold. We hunger for anything which might seem a more direct communication from God, which might bring clarity to our search, validate our path, provide some certitude in our cryptic world.

No one in the Carmelite tradition had as much to say about extraordinary experiences as Teresa of Avila and John of the Cross. Earlier Carmelites claimed that Mary, the Mother of God, appeared to one of the thirteenth century generals of the order, Simon Stock, and promised to protect the order. However, the earliest accounts of this vision come from the fourteenth century. St. Mary Magdalene de' Pazzi, a Carmelite nun in Florence (d. 1604) experienced powerful visions and ecstacies which caused her, at times, to remain motionless, and at other times to move about pantomiming the vision.[1]

However, it was the Spanish mystics who introduced paranormal experiences so vividly into the tradition, and who attempted a systematic analysis of these experiences. These saints had helpful instructions for the ordinary life of all Christians, but often their works were seen as guides for those unusual times when Christians were undergoing odd happenings. Then, one might take these works off the shelf and dare approach this dangerous material. But until one had such experiences, or was trying to assist someone else having such experiences, it was thought better to approach these works through secondary sources, the writings of experts who could give guidance.

To be fair, Teresa of Avila and John of the Cross did not emphasize the extraordinary; as a matter of fact they downplayed these phenomena. John was quite circumspect, and Teresa said the only important thing was to do God's will.

Today, we see the mystics not as an esoteric group of Christians having experiences not available to the rest of us, but as "pioneers of humanity," clarifiers of what it means to be human, paradigms of humanity. They were writing about the full flowering of the baptismal promises made by every Christian. The extraordinary experiences were seen for what they were: secondary phenomena which occasionally occurred in the lives of some of the mystics, but were not of the essence of the spiritual journey, and were certainly not the goal.

In our more psychologically sophisticated era, questions have been raised about the authenticity of much of what the mystics reported. The visions and so forth perhaps said less about God, and more about the frail human psyche which was straining under the effort of relating to the divine.

Also, we realize some of the accounts were written by people who had a stake in sensationalizing the lives of these saints in order to have them recognized by the church. Then, too, as stories are repeated they tend to become more sensational. One nun in the Incarnation in Avila reported that when Teresa and John were conversing about the Trinity they simultaneously went into an ecstasy. Her account was fairly general. When this event was later painted, both of them are seen levitating in the air, as well as the chair John was sitting on–which could lead to a first law of levitation: anything you are touching goes up when you do. But it may say more about the imagination of the painter than anything about suspension of the law of gravity.

So, for many reasons the accent has been off the unusual in mystics such as Teresa and John, and focus has been on their teachings which are of benefit to all Christians. And yet, these experiences and their discussions about such experiences sit there in the writings of Teresa and John. They obviously gave a good deal of thought to them, and were forced to come to terms with them in their own lives, and in the lives of other Christians.

Today, people frequently report extraordinary experiences. Rather than be embarrassed about the reports of the mystics, we may be able to learn from them attitudes appropriate to our own searching era. The time for visions and voices has apparently not passed.

The "Supernatural"

John of the Cross identified as "supernatural" any knowledge or communication coming to a person outside the normal manner. He writes:

> Our discussion...will deal only with the supernatural knowledge which reaches the intellect by way of the exterior bodily senses (sight, hearing, smell, taste, and touch). Through these senses, spiritual persons can and usually do perceive supernatural representations and objects.
>
> As for sight, they are wont to have visions of

> images and persons from the other life: of saints, of the good and bad angels, and of unusual lights and splendors.
>
> Through hearing they apprehend certain extraordinary words, sometimes from the vision, and at other times without seeing the one who speaks.
>
> With the sense of smell they sometimes notice sensibly the sweetest fragrances without knowledge of their origin.
>
> Also it happens in regard to taste that they experience very exquisite savors.
>
> And concerning touch they feel extreme delight, at times so intense that all the bones and marrow rejoice, flourish, and bathe in it. This delight is usually termed spiritual unction, because in pure souls it passes from the spirit to the senses. The experience is common with spiritual persons. It is an overflow from the affection and devotion of the sensible spirit, which each person receives in their own way.[2]

It is clear that John of the Cross assumes that God often assists a person's spiritual journey with supernatural communication. He described the manner in which God ordinarily proceeds: First, God uses natural exterior objects such as sermons, masses, holy objects, and penances. Then God may present a supernatural favor such as a vision of a saint.

Meanwhile, the interior senses of imagination and fantasy are using meditation and reasoning for the instruction of the spirit. At the proper time God may assist these interior senses with supernatural imaginative visions.

John admits God does not always follow this procedure, but "[God's] ordinary procedure conforms with our explanation."[3]

When speaking about these supernatural experiences, Teresa and John generally grouped them into three categories. Visions may be described as corporeal, imaginative, or intellectual.

The visions that are corporeal, or physical, apparently take place in the outer environment and are observed by the physical senses. These visions are seen with the eyes, heard with the ears and so forth.

The imaginative visions are not seen or heard in the environment with the physical senses, but these visions take place within the interior space of the psyche, in the imagination. And although they are called imaginative visions the mystic is adamant that he or she is not simply imagining something. They claim to be receiving a communication of some sort.

The intellectual visions are the most interior and usually are understood to have neither form nor image. Even though they are called visions, they are actually intuitive understandings, generally beyond any specific reporting.

In the estimation of these Carmelites, the more exterior and concrete or physical a vision is, the less trustworthy. The more interior and formless, the more trustworthy.

Corporeal Visions

Corporeal visions seen or heard with the bodily eyes or ears apparently were quite rare. Teresa had numerous visions of Christ and she said she did not think any of those visions were corporeal. Although, one time while praying to Christ she heard an indistinct voice with her bodily ears.[4] Her visions of Christ were always imaginative or intellectual; in other words, they took place inside her, not outside in her environment.

One time a devil sat on Teresa's prayer book so she could not finish her prayers.[5] One would think the vision were corporeal, but in reporting it, she said that this one had no physical form, but she admits that sometimes she did see a physical form. Such reports were rare and the mystics were quite wary of them. Teresa believed that such visions could be produced by God or by the devil, or the person could just be delusional.

John of the Cross is adamant about these corporeal visions or locutions: *never rely on them or accept them.* Do not even try to discern whether they are good or bad; consider them diabolical. His reasoning is that if they are diabolical they will cause unrest; if they are from God they have already produced their effect without depending upon our discernment. It is simply safer to pay no attention. John is always concerned that we do not stop with the form or image but continue to be led into the mystery of God. The more concrete the image, the more suspicious is John, and the greater the possibility of inauthenticity. I am reminded of the following personal experience: An elderly man whom I know quite well told me about a vision he had when he was younger. It was obviously a moving religious experience and he speaks of it as a great grace which gave him peace. He had been injured in an accident and was recuperating in a hospital. At the time, he was quite concerned about a friend of his who was in serious trouble with the law. While he was lying in the hospital bed he began praying for his friend. As he prayed fervently, St. Thérèse, the Little Flower, appeared at the foot of the bed. And he told me, "I saw her just as clearly as I see you now...the brown habit, white cloak, roses. And she spoke to me, and I heard her as clearly as we are speaking. She said to me, 'Go back to sleep, he's not worth it.'"

Theologian Karl Rahner would have sympathy with this story. He pointed out the complexity of such an event: first, there is the core religious experience; then, you have a description of it; and then, the interpretation of it.

John of the Cross knew that accurately assessing such an experience is a slippery process. He identified six kinds of problems that may occur if one accepts visions, authentic or not: first, faith diminishes as the senses feast; second, visions keep the spirit from soaring; third, the person becomes possessive; fourth, visions gradually lose their effect because the soul attends only to the sensible aspect; fifth, God's favor is lost as the soul assumes the communication to be its own; sixth, visions open the door to the devil, who is a good counterfeiter.[6]

Imaginative Visions

The preponderance of extraordinary experiences of Teresa of Avila were imaginative, or psychological; that is, they took place within the mystic, within her consciousness, and not outside in the physical environment. For example, one of Teresa's more vivid visions was of her place in hell:

> ...While I was in prayer one day I suddenly found that, without knowing how, I had seemingly been put in hell. I understood that the Lord wanted me to see the place the devils had prepared there for me and which I merited because of my sins. This experience took place within the shortest space of time, but even were I to live for many years I think it would be impossible for me to forget it.
>
> The entrance it seems to me was similar to a very long and narrow alleyway, like an oven, low and dark and confined; the floor seemed to consist of dirty, muddy water emitting a foul stench and swarming with putrid vermin. At the end of the alleyway a hole that looked like a small cupboard was hollowed out in the wall; there I found I was placed in a cramped condition. All of this was delightful to see in comparison with what I felt there. What I have described can hardly be exaggerated.[7]

Teresa considered this vision a great grace. It lessened her fear of trials in this life and gave her strength to suffer them. It was one of the experiences which led to a conversion in her life, and eventually, to a reform of the Carmelites.

On another occasion she saw an angel at her side, with a large golden dart. The pointed tip of the dart had a small flame, and the angel plunged the dart several times into her heart. "When he drew it out, I thought he was carrying off with him the deepest part of me; and he left me all on fire with great love of God."[8] This vision, captured in a sculpture by Bernini, has entered the Christian imagination.

The tremendous task of beginning the reform and founding a new type of community was supported by visions. Teresa reports an imaginative vision of St. Joseph, who encouraged her to hire workmen even though she had no money at the time. A beautiful St. Clare appeared and urged her to proceed with courage. Our Lady appeared and assured her of success. "It seemed to me she placed around my neck a very beautiful golden necklace to which was attached a highly valuable cross."[9] The Franciscan friar, Peter of Alcantara, whom Teresa consulted while he was alive, appeared to her several times after his death, one time urging her not to accept income for her new convents.[10] Jesus and Mary appeared and expressed approval of Teresa's first foundation.[11] On the feast of Pentecost she saw a dove over her head. In place of feathers, its wings were made of brilliant shells. As usual, Teresa could report an effect in her life: "I noted from that day the greatest improvement in myself brought about by a more sublime love of God and much stronger virtues."[12]

The positive side of imaginative visions, in Teresa's estimation, is that at least we are seeing and hearing something in accord with our nature. For example, Teresa said, it is very beneficial when our Lord shows his most sacred humanity clearly to a person as he was when on earth or is now in heaven.

In her own experience Christ showed her his humanity little by little, beginning with the hands. She eventually realized why she could not see him entirely: "So much glory would have been unbearable next to so lowly and wretched a subject as I; and as one who knew this, the merciful Lord was preparing me."[13] Four times she had a vision of the humanity of Christ "taken into the bosom of the Father." She considered these striking visions the most sublime she ever received.[14] They were strongly engraved on her imagination.

She realized the devil could counterfeit certain imaginative visions, but even then, good may result. She counseled that even if the devil is able to produce in our imagination an image of Christ, we should still reverence it. A painter may be a poor painter, but we can still reverence the image.

She herself had received advice to the contrary at one time in her life. When she was reporting her visions of Christ to her confessor, he feared it was from the devil. He advised her not to reverence the vision, but on the contrary, give it the "fig," a gesture of scorn.[15] The advice caused Teresa great difficulty. Here is our Lord, she reflected, who suffered so much for us in his lifetime and on the cross, and is now favoring her by appearing to her, and she in return is giving him the "fig." Although she was under obedience and believed the Lord would understand, in her heart of hearts she felt it was not right. The image should have been reverenced, even if it were from the devil.

In the same imaginative or psychological category, Teresa also spoke about receiving locutions. She believed that the locutions from God can be distinguished from the diabolical, or ones produced by our imagination. True locutions, she wrote, will have these signs: they will have power and authority, for locutions from God affect what they say; the soul is left in great quiet, in devout and peaceful recollection, with a readiness to praise God; the words remain in the memory for a long time, and some are never forgotten. The thought remains that, no matter what, in the end these words will be accomplished.[16]

Teresa observed that locutions from sources other than God have none of these signs: neither certitude, nor peace, nor interior delight. She doubts that anyone with experience of God's locutions will be deceived by the imagination.

The devil is trickier, and if something is to be done as a result of a locution, it should be told to someone who is a prudent confessor and servant of God. John of the Cross concurs. His reasoning is, where two or three are gathered, there Christ is in their midst.

On several occasions, Teresa was tormented with visions of the devil:

> I was once in an oratory, and he appeared to me in an abominable form at my left side. Because he spoke to me, I looked particularly at his mouth—which was frightening. It seemed that a great flame, all bright without shadow, came forth from his body. He told me in a terrifying way that I had really freed myself from his hands but that he would catch me with them again. I was struck with great fear and blessed myself as best I could; he disappeared, but returned right away. This happened to me twice. I didn't know what to do. There was some holy water there, and I threw it in that direction; he never returned again.[17]

In her experience, the devils fled from a cross, but returned; holy water had more power in scattering them.

While some visions may have been frightening, Teresa learned from the Lord not to fear the devils. They had no real power over her. She became bold and challenged them: "'Come now all of you, for, being a servant of the Lord, I want to see what you can do to me.'"[18]

She learned that the real demonic is found in our own attachments to what is contrary to God and God's will. The devils are powerful, she learned, only when we are being a devil to ourselves, when we are in contradiction with ourselves. But those who embrace the cross and serve God have nothing to fear. She concluded, "I don't understand these fears, 'The devil! The devil!', when we can say 'God!' 'God!', and make the devil tremble."[19] As a matter of fact, those who feared the devil frightened her more than did the devil.

Teresa observed that a good sign of authentic visions is increasing humility: "...when the Spirit is from God the soul esteems itself less...."[20] She warned against overestimating oneself just because one is receiving locutions. Remember, she said, God also spoke to the Pharisees!

Even though Teresa believed that these imaginative visions were generally a great grace for her, still, she said, one should not desire them. She enumerated her reasons: it shows a lack of humility to want what you have never earned; the devil can play a thousand tricks; the imagination itself can see what it wants to see, e.g. in a dream at night after thinking about it during the day; it is bold to choose a path not knowing if one is suited for it; trials may come with visions, and the question will be, can you bear them? Teresa concluded: "...the safest way is to want only what God wants....So there are many holy persons who have never received one of these favors; and others who receive them but are not holy."[21]

John of the Cross had no interest in discerning good visions from bad visions. Ignore and reject them all, he advised. He saw plenty of evidence of imaginative visions in scripture, for example, in the visions of Isaiah, Jeremiah, Daniel, and the dream of Pilate's wife. But, in his estimation, any vision is always limited in mode and manner and cannot adequately represent God's wisdom. If visions are truly from God no resistance is possible and they produce their good effect in the soul regardless.

John's basic advice concerning corporeal and imaginative visions is that they must all be renounced. When they are from God they inevitably benefit the soul. By distancing itself from visions, the soul safeguards the true purpose of the visions, which is to engender a spirit of devotion.

John also counsels the spiritual director to ignore the visions. The director should not make the visions a topic of conversation, nor should the director show esteem for them. Any curiosity may cause the individual to overestimate the visions.

Even visions and locutions from God can mislead, says John: in the first place, the true meaning is not always found in the literal meaning; and secondly, people and times change, so the communications become flexible (e.g., something predicted does not happen because people have repented.) John related to his beloved brother, Francisco, his own experience of a locution. Francisco gave the following report:

> While Father Fray John was in Segovia as superior he sent for me here [Medina]. I went to see him, and after having been there two or three days, I asked to return. He asked me to stay for some more days because he didn't know when we would see each other again. This was the last time I saw him. After supper one evening, he took me by the hand and brought me to the garden and while we were there alone he told me: "I want to tell you something that happened to me with our Lord. We had a crucifix in the monastery and while I was there before it one day, it occurred to me that it belonged more appropriately in the church because I didn't want it venerated only by the friars but also by outsiders. So I carried out my idea. After having placed it in the church as respectably as I could, I was one day praying before it and Christ said to me: Fray John, ask whatever you want, for I will grant your request because of this service you have rendered me. I told him: Lord,

> give me trials to suffer for you, that I may be despised and held in no account. I asked this of our Lord, and His Majesty has so changed things that I am sorry over all the honor I'm shown without meriting it."[22]

John believed that when a vision is from God, it contains an inclination to consult appropriate people. "God will not bring clarification and confirmation of the truth to the heart of one who is alone."[23] One should tell supernatural visions to the spiritual director in full. But the director "should explain how one act done in charity is more precious in God's sight than all the visions and communications possible...and how is it that many individuals who have not received these experiences are incomparably more advanced than others who have received many."[24]

In general, John believed that an emphasis on extraordinary experiences violates the spirit of Christianity. He even said it was offensive to God. And John put these words in God's mouth:

> If I have already told you all things in My Word, my Son, and if I have no other word, what answer or revelation can I now make that would surpass this? Fasten your eyes on Him alone, because in Him I have spoken and revealed all, and in Him you will discover even more than you ask for and desire. You are making an appeal for locutions, and revelations, that are incomplete, but if you turn your eyes to Him you will find them complete. For He is My entire locution and response, vision and revelation, which I have already spoken, answered, manifested, and revealed to you, by giving Him to you as a brother, companion, master, ransom, and reward.[25]

John taught that one should believe only the teachings of Christ and Christ's ministers.

Intellectual Visions

Intellectual visions are a third type identified by the mystics. These are the most interior. John defines intellectual visions as knowledge immediately present to the intellect without any mediation of the senses, outer or inner.

Teresa described her first experience of an intellectual vision: "Being in prayer on the feastday of the glorious St. Peter, I saw or, to put it better, I felt Christ beside me; I saw nothing with my bodily eyes or with my soul, but it seemed to me that Christ was at my side—I saw that it was He, in my opinion, who was speaking to me."[26] She said that such a vision may last many days, perhaps more than a year. In her own experience she felt he was walking at her right side. The presence at her side could also be the Blessed Mother, or a saint.

Both saints report that an intellectual vision comes from such intimate depths that there is certitude it is not from the devil or the imagination. Teresa, for example, observed that a locution accompanying an intellectual vision had distinct characteristics: first, it is clear; second, it comes unexpectedly, often when one is not thinking about what one hears; third the locution comes as something *heard*; whereas when it is from one's imagination it appears *composed*; fourth, a great deal is immediately comprehended, whereas the intellect on its own could not compose so quickly; fifth, together with the words much more is given than ever dreamed of without words.[27]

John of the Cross identified four types of intellectual visions, which he called "visions of the soul": visions, revelations, locutions, and feelings. His general recommendation is to disregard them and do not desire them.

However, in two instances John does *not* recommend rejection. One should attend to an "intellectual substantial locution" which brings about what it expresses in the substance of the soul. His example is, if the locution were, "Be good," the soul would then be substantially good. Nor should one reject a revelation which offers intellectual knowledge about God. This revelation is pure contemplation, union with God, a touch of divinity. "The soul should rather be resigned and humble about them."[28] One can do nothing about such experiences anyway.

At times these locutions and visions powerfully affect the senses. Teresa speaks of raptures, ecstasy, and transport, which are all the same to her. It may be a word which brings the person into suspension. But at other times, through an intellectual vision, there is a suspension and the soul does not know how to speak of it.

If there is no image and faculties do not understand, how can the visions be remembered? "I don't understand this either," says Teresa. She said it was like going into the Duchess of Alba's house, seeing everything, but remembering nothing specific.[29] Sometimes in the ecstasy, the breath is taken away, no speech is possible, and sometimes the hands and the body grow cold. This extreme intensity does not last long.[30]

She also speaks about a powerful rapture she calls the "flight of the spirit." Teresa attempted to describe it: "It is such that the spirit truly seems to go forth from the body. On the other hand, it is clear that this person is not dead; at least, he cannot say whether for some moments he was in the body or not. It seems to him that he was entirely in another region different from this in which we live...."[31] The soul is carried off like a giant snatching a straw, or a huge wave lifting a little ship. During this time she received imaginative and intellectual visions. The effects she reports here are: a knowledge of the grandeur of God, a self-knowledge and humility, and a lessening of esteem for earthly things, except those which can be used for the service of God.

The Carmelite Contribution

What are we to make of these visions today, in our more skeptical age? Or are we more skeptical? People continue to report seeing extraordinary sights, for example, weeping statues of Mary, blood running, the face of Jesus.

In discussing their visions and voices, Teresa and John were obviously convinced that certain experiences were truly from God. In Teresa's estimation they were great favors which strengthened her, encouraged her, confirmed her direction, freed her, took away fear, made her faith more lively and her life more generous.

Nor could Teresa be accused of being gullible. If anything, she was hard-headed when it came to discerning authentic from inauthentic prayer experiences. Rather than raising expectations of rapture and ecstasy, Teresa counseled her sisters to value ordinary duties, even if time-consuming. She reminded them that "the Lord walks among the pots and pans...."[32] Her superiors were to praise their sisters for humility, mortification, and obedience, more than for "supernatural" experiences. She was suspicious of nuns who spent long hours in a daze, ostensibly favored by God. She recommended they be given duties to distract them.

One time a confessor asked Teresa's advice about a person who claimed to have visions of Mary. The person said that Our Lady sat on her bed, spoke to her at great length, and told her about the future. "So I told him to wait to see if the prophecies would prove true," wrote Teresa, "and to look for other effects and inquire into the life of that person. In the end he came to understand that the whole thing was nonsense."[33]

And yet, as we listen to her accounts, her own visions often seem to be highly conditioned by psychological and sociological factors. For example, in the early stages of the reform, when Teresa was feeling intense pressures, her visions were quite numerous; she sees the devil as the devil was portrayed in her times; she has a vision of certain religious orders battling "heretics," as the Reformation proponents would have been understood; she even saw Jesuits in heaven.

Theologian Karl Rahner, who was instrumental in the resurgence of studies of the mystics, believed that these mystics were the same as we are, not a different breed of humanity. He holds that the mystics are like us in kind but not in degree. They have the same humanity we have, the same basic psychological structure, but their particular sensitivity to the transcendent and the intensity of their religious experiences set them apart. It is interesting to note that as union with God deepens, extraordinary experiences begin to disappear. What remains is the ordinary, loved and served.

Is it possible that everything these mystics report is naturally explainable? Could John be wrong in calling them "supernatural," in other words, inexplicable by normal processes? Certainly there are many things we understand in science today which would have been beyond comprehension in the time of John and Teresa. We know so little about the human psyche and its powers. Our present day self-consciousness itself is quite recent in the long history of evolution. We do not know the extent of our physical powers. We are at the edges of our experience in dealing with chakras, auras, and the various forms of energy.

If we were able to explain the mystical phenomena naturally, would that reduce them to "nothing but" psychological processes, sociological conditioning, or other perfectly understandable processes? Not necessarily. If this world is graced with God's presence and power then ordinary processes, in themselves quite understandable, can still be powerful communications from God acting through secondary sources. They are direct experiences of God, but mediated.

One of the more helpful explanations of secondary phenomena understands them as the spillover of God's activity in a person's life. God's loving self-communication at the core of a person's being reverberates through the various levels of the body-person, including the psychological and the physical. These are highly conditioned responses on various levels to the impact of this graciousness in the center of our being. The image and the word become a momentary form of grace.

Teresa and John certainly understood extraordinary experiences as direct interventions from God. We would want to stay open to that possibility lest we limit God's freedom. And the very nature of Christianity understood as an historically revealed religion argues for the possibility of God's intervention in the world. Even given the possibility of such experiences, a healthy skepticism is probably safer than a naive credulity.

But it is possible to argue that God is already thoroughly implicated in the world; that the ordinary is itself already extraordinary. This world is not something God is doing as an extra project, as though God's real life were elsewhere. This world is manifesting God's very life and essence which is to create, to bring to life, to love. God's Spirit is at the heart of this world loving it in a continuing creation. We are truly seeing God in this creation and therefore it is *all* a vision, a locution, a fragrance, a taste, a touch. It is all divine; it is all natural.

For example, are the extraordinary religious experiences which are happening in various places in the world today only available in those places?[34] People are certainly to be believed when they say they have had powerful religious experiences and that they have undergone conversions. But could it be that particular constellations of factors, all of which can be explained naturally, are putting people in touch with the transcendent which is offered to all, everywhere, but usually only known implicitly? Is it possible that these special places on the earth make explicit the Mystery which is always present to us, inviting us into a relationship? May not any bush, through the eyes of faith, be the burning bush? If Medjugorje, then why not Mishawaka?

Teresa said in these matters of visions and voices it is safest to want only what God wants. And John of the Cross said let none of it distract us from our relationship with Christ and our ordinary life of faith. The impact of these Carmelite mystics on the order and the church enables many more of us to be seers, to come to an awareness in our lives that we are continually seeing, touching, tasting God. Teresa and John open us to the transcendent in everyday life. And through these everyday visions we are offered a love which is divinizing us so that we become for one another a more and more transparent vision of God.

NOTES

1. For a brief account of the life of Mary Magdalene de' Pazzi cf. Joachim Smet, *The Carmelites*, 2 (Darien, IL: Carmelite Spiritual Center, 1976), 217-221.

2. John of the Cross, *The Ascent of Mount Carmel*, in *The Collected Works of St. John of the Cross*, trans. Kieran Kavanaugh, O.C.D., and Otilio Rodriguez, O.C.D. (Washington, D.C.: ICS Publications, 1991) Book 2, chap. 11, no. 1. John says that sometimes these people smell sweet fragrances. But, apparently, not all supernatural fragrances are so sweet. When Teresa was having trouble getting rid of devils she called for the sisters to bring her holy water. "I called for holy water, and those who entered after the devil had already gone (for they were two nuns well worthy of belief, who would by no means tell a lie) smelled a foul stench like that of brimstone. I didn't smell it. It so lingered that one could notice it."

Teresa of Avila, *Life,* in *The Collected Works of St. Teresa of Avila,* 1, trans. Kieran Kavanaugh, O.C.D., and Otilio Rodriguez, O.C.D. (Washington, D.C.: ICS Publications, 1976), chap. 31, no. 6.

3. John of the Cross, *The Ascent of Mount Carmel,* Book Two, chap. 17, nos. 3, 4.

4. Teresa of Avila, *Life,* chap. 39, 3.

5. Ibid., chap. 31, no. 10.

6. John of the Cross, *The Ascent of Mount Carmel* , Book Two, chap. 11, no. 7.

7. Teresa of Avila, *Life* , chap. 32, no. 1.

8. Ibid., chap. 29, no. 13.

9. Ibid., chap. 33, no. 14.

10. Ibid., chap. 36, no. 20.

11. Ibid., no. 24.

12. Ibid. chap. 38, no. 11.

13. Ibid., chap. 28, no. 1.

14. Ibid., chap. 38, no. 18.

15. The "fig" was apparently made by placing the thumb between the first two fingers and holding it at the end of the nose.

16. Teresa of Avila, *Interior Castle,* in *The Collected Works of St. Teresa of Avila,* 2, The Sixth Dwelling Places, chap. 3, nos. 5–8.

17. Teresa of Avila, *Life,* chap. 31, no. 2.

18. Ibid., chap. 25, no. 19.

19. Ibid., no. 22.

20. Ibid., *Interior Castle,* The Sixth Dwelling Places, chap. 3, no. 17.

21. Ibid., chap. 9, no 16.

22. Federico Ruiz, O.C.D., et al., *God Speaks in the Night,* trans. Kieran Kavanaugh, O.C.D. (Washington, D.C.: ICS Publications, 1991), 341.

23. John of the Cross, *The Ascent of Mount Carmel,* Book Two, chap. 22, no. 11.

24. Ibid., no. 19.

25. Ibid., no. 5.

26. Teresa of Avila, *Life,* chap. 27, no. 2.

27. Teresa of Avila, *The Interior Castle,* The Sixth Dwelling Places, chap. 3, nos. 12f.

28. John of the Cross, *The Ascent of Mount Carmel,* Book Two, chap. 31, no. 2.

29. Teresa of Avila, *The Interior Castle,* The Sixth Dwelling Places, chap. 4, no. 8.

30. Ibid., no. 13.

31. Ibid., chap. 5, no. 7.

32. Teresa of Avila, *The Foundations*, in *The Collected Works of St. Teresa of Avila,* 3, chap. 5, no. 8.

33. Ibid., chap 8, no. 7.

34. Lourdes and Fatima are among the places that come immediately to mind. The Marian apparitions in these two places, and in a very few others, have been approved by the church as credible but not as objects of Catholic doctrine. For a brief discussion of visions, cf. John Welch, "Visions," in *Encyclopedia of Catholicism*, ed. Richard P. McBrien (HarperSanFrancisco, 1995), 1317.

Chapter Nine

CONTEMPLATION AND COMPASSION

The Tradition as Resource for Justice and Peace

If a tradition of spirituality had nothing to say to a world which is mostly poor and in which great injustice occurs, then it would merely be a museum piece. In recent decades, the Catholic Church has increasingly called attention to the enormous problem of the world's social inequities, and challenged Christians to work for a more just world.[1]

The essence of Carmelite spirituality is "allegiance to Jesus Christ." The church was born from the mission of Christ which was taken up by his followers. It was a mission of evangelization, spreading the good news of God's nearness and love for each one. Today the church is calling for a *new evangelization*. This new mission is a continuation of the original mission, to bring the message and values of the gospel to all peoples and all parts of society. This gospel is preached for the transformation in Christ of the whole world.[2]

The leaders of the Carmelite Orders are calling for a *new spirituality* to accompany the new evangelization. It is the spirituality of the first Carmelites, and of Teresa and John, and all contributors to the tradition, but heard in a new key. The new spirituality is to be born from the encounter of this eight hundred-year-old tradition with the overwhelming plight of a majority of the world's inhabitants.

In the struggle for a more just and peaceful world, the Carmelite tradition has been identified by many as a rich resource. Aram, a lay associate of the Carmelites in the Philippines, writes:

> With our experience of involvement in the work of justice and liberation, where focus is on the outer world of history, we feel the indispensability of interiority, the inner self, the inner strength, the inner journey to sustain us, to keep us from being burnt-out, to help us be deepened in spirit and in the ways of the Lord. It is I think this particular charism of the Carmelites that I think has attracted lay people involved in the social movement to relate with the Order and to identify with this search and process.[3]

The "Idyllic" First Community

The peaceful hermits of Carmel camped in a wadi in the middle of armed Crusaders and Saracens who were dressed in the armor and accoutrements of war. Within the wadi the hermits were donning the armor of faith. Around them Crusaders and Muslim warriors contested control of the Holy Land. Within the wadi, God's *shalom* accompanied their quiet life.

For the first one hundred years of the order's existence Carmelites silently worked and prayed in this canyon on Mount Carmel, even while members were slowly migrating to Europe. In the memory of the order, this brief period became the golden period of the Carmelite ideal. It was Carmel's version of the nascent Christian community described in the Acts of the Apostles. The ideals of peace and justice were associated with the mountain and with the Carmelite community on the mountain.

A mythic, idyllic community, led by the prophet Elijah, is depicted in that important fourteenth-century spiritual document of the Carmelites, *The Institution of the First Monks*. This work has a unique interpretation of Elijah's experience in the cave on Mount Horeb. The "gentle air" signifies that God has assigned Elijah a peace-keeping role. He is to gather faithful disciples who have been suffering persecution and bring them to a place of peace. This man of peace brings them to Mount Carmel. The community on the mountain is uniquely faithful to God, and, because of its faithfulness, it is spared the Babylonian captivity.

The author of the *Institution* applied the prophecy of Isaiah to this community on Mount Carmel:

> As the Prophet Isaias, in the person of the Lord, foretold about them and their dwelling place: "Judgment shall dwell in the wilderness, and justice shall sit in Carmel, and the work of justice shall be peace, and the service of justice, quietness, and security forever. And my people shall sit in the beauty of peace, and in the tabernacles of confidence, and in wealthy rest" (Is 32:16–18).[4]

In this way the Carmelite imagination has amplified the original setting of the first generation of Carmelites with a mythic earlier settlement built on the deeds and person of Elijah. The place of the Carmelites becomes interiorized. The origins thus become a rich source for establishing the essential identity of the Carmelite, as well as perennial Carmelite themes, including the theme of a life of justice which results in God's peace.

Listening

A foundational theme running throughout the Carmelite tradition is that of listening, being attentive. Any life, any work on behalf of people, begins by asking, "What is God doing?" Before any of our activity, God is at work approaching our world with a life-giving love. Over and over the Carmelite tradition encourages an awareness of the presence of this Mystery and a receptivity to the demands of such love. In other words, the work of justice begins in contemplation.

If contemplation may be understood as an openness to God's transforming love, no matter how God is approaching us, then it is a foundational human activity. It will do no good to build our kingdoms if they are not also on the way to being God's kingdom.

The traditional values of silence and solitude, recommended to the first Carmelites in their Rule, were not meant to isolate the men or lead them to self-absorption. Silence and solitude are essential conditions for listening. Teresa of Avila complained that preoccupations in her life made such a clamor that it was difficult to hear the gentle whistle of the shepherd emanating from the center of her castle. Silence and solitude become interior conditions which make all the activity and work of our lives porous to God's spirit.

Aram comments on the Rule of Carmel which speaks of a cell, silence, and solitude:

> I work in the hinterlands among the farmers and farm workers on the island of Samar and I do not have a cell I can call my own, because our work necessitates that we live among the people, eat with them, sleep in their huts, work with them. But as I walk from one barrio to another, cross rivers and traverse mountains, I take that time of solitude to confront silence.[5]

It is in contemplative prayer that our lives slowly change to conform to God's will. If we may understand God's will to be the well-being of humanity, then growing in accord with God's will means that the life and work of the Christian are more and more aware of, and responsive to, the lives of those whose well-being is under constant assault. A ministry grounded on such foundations will have the best chance to bear the fruits of a peaceful and just world.

Keeping the Center Open

Idolatry is not the result of people obstinately choosing that which is obviously false. Idolatry is usually the result of something good being exalted beyond its value. It is a good carried to an extreme, and thereby distorted. It is a good, become a god. The charism of the Carmelites calls for continual vigilance lest our good intentions and activities unwittingly create idols.

A constant admonition from the Carmelite saints is to *keep the center open*. "The soul's center is God," writes John of the Cross. It is there, at the center, that the human spirit and the spirit of God meet and burn into one flame. Because God at the center of our existence is the Mystery who is no one and no thing (*nada*!), we are always catching mere glints of God's presence in the concreteness of creation.

> All who are free
> tell me a thousand graceful things of you;
> all wound me more
> and leave me dying
> of, ah, I-don't-know-what behind their stammering.[6]

John of the Cross, in these beautiful lines from *The Spiritual Canticle*, acknowledges that this world introduces God to us. We find traces of God's passing in its fascination.

But, what introduces God to us very quickly becomes confused with God. We fill in the center with something or someone and ask it to be the fulfillment of all our desires. We attempt to quench our thirst for the infinite with something finite. When this happens, we terribly distort whatever it is we are asking to be our god. No one, and nothing, can bear that responsibility and so we begin to squeeze the life out of our loves. And we die, too, because we need the nourishment only God can give. A lesser god means a lesser self.

In intense situations of extreme need where people are trying to be faithful ministers of the gospel, the very movement or activity on behalf of justice may *fill-in the center*. Seemingly beneficent entities such as a particular political party, a certain leader, a specific strategy, a vision of a hoped-for outcome, even "the people," have the potential to take God's place in the center. Total dedication to "the people" may unwittingly mask a lack of prayer, and therefore an inattentiveness to God.

In the struggle for justice we may begin to assume we know what God wants, and begin to act with the assumption that what we want, God wants. Therefore, we struggle mightily for what *we* want. John of the Cross always suspects that we measure God by ourselves, rather than ourselves by God. The unintended result of our idolatry may be harm done to the very people and causes we are attempting to serve. Aram comments from her experience in the Philippines:

> I feel that Carmel offers to nurture us in the spirit of service. As leaders of our own people, we remain as servants–so that the sense of service is not corrupted; so that the social movement does not only replace structures and systems and leaders with others who would do the same as their predecessors, but with those who remain dedicated servants of God.
>
> It is this contemplative component of Carmel that attracts a number of committed and dedicated leaders and workers in *cause oriented groups* in our country to Carmelite spirituality.[7]

A traditional Carmelite expression for keeping the center open is "purity of heart." This theme signifies a detachment from idols, a liberation of a heart too easily enslaved. In *The Institution of the First Monks* "purity of heart" emerged as a theme linking Elijah and Mary. In this work, Elijah is portrayed as the first man to take a vow of virginity, and Mary is the first woman to take a vow of virginity. These foundational figures in the Carmelite tradition represent an openness to God's activity. They are "free for God"; they live in expectation of God's will, allowing no one and nothing to defile their hearts.

Such detachment, such "purity of heart" calls for human effort but is ultimately the work of God. John of the Cross observes that lesser loves attract us with such power that only a deeper, more powerful love kindled in our lives can lead us past where we have become stuck. In the presence of this love, lesser loves melt away. What was impossible to do ascetically by sheer willpower, now becomes possible as the heart is lured into the wilderness of God.

Nonetheless, the work of justice calls for a disciplined life in which asceticism and self-denial have a necessary place. As

Chilean writer Segundo Galilea commented, "...there is no real human development (liberation) without a collectively embraced asceticism, renunciation and austerity."[8] We need this vigilance because there is an ambiguity about life and about our intentions. Something in us wants to close us in on ourselves, to turn all things and everyone to our advantage. We have a tendency to deny our rootedness in God and to assume an independent, self-sustained posture. The ascetical principles found in Carmelite writings war against the subtle forms of slavery and selfishness.

Fortunately for us, God meets us where we are. Teresa of Avila, on one occasion, found John of the Cross too demanding. He counseled that a soul needs to be "dead to the world" to find God. Teresa playfully countered that such a search would be too costly, and is unnecessary as well. She pointed to the women in the Bible: "The Magdalene was not dead to the world when she found him, nor was the Samaritan woman or the Canaanite woman....God deliver me from people so spiritual that they want to turn everything into perfect contemplation, no matter what."[9] Our challenge, says Teresa, is to *meet* God's acceptance of us.

Meanwhile, with freer hearts, people live and work and wait in hope. Aram from the Philippines writes:

> In the basic Christian communities, people silently work in preparation of the Coming–not sure when the change will happen, not sure when the promise will be realized. But they keep the *hope*. They organize, they study the situation, they act, they pray. They keep the faith and that keeps them struggling and dreaming for a better life for everyone. *Let then contemplation become a source of strength rather than of passive waiting.* [10]

Living in the Midst of the People

The Carmelite tradition was born in the hearts of those who heard an invitation from God, and followed it. The first invitation was into solitude with like-minded brothers. The second invitation was into the urban life of Europe, to serve the *minores*, the poor of the new cities, as well as the emerging middle class. The apostolic life chosen by the Carmelites eventually led them into the universities and into all levels of the church and society.[11] Following further invitations, the order spread from Europe into numerous mission lands.[12] Over five hundred years ago Carmelites entered Brazil and Latin America, beginning a long relationship between these peoples and the Carmelite tradition.[13] The settings in which the Carmelite tradition has been lived have impacted the spirituality of Carmel. It is a spirituality that can speak to all types of people, in all lifestyles, in all levels of society.

One of the modifications of the Carmelite Rule in 1247 allowed the one-time hermits to accept new foundations *where they are given*. Some commentators on the tradition find in this attitude a willingness to be led by God's people to places not of the Carmelite's own choosing. He or she is disposable, free for God.

Today, the Carmelite Orders, following the church, have called their members to a preferential option for the poor. Living "in the midst of the people," as Carmelite documents urge, will result in a *new experience* of the living God.[14] John of the Cross noted that a prayerful union with God does not remove one from the world's concerns, but drives one "deep into the thicket" of the world's suffering.

> Let us rejoice, Beloved,
> and let us go forth to behold
> ourselves in your beauty,
> to the mountain and to the hill,
> to where the pure water flows,
> and further, deep into the thicket.[15]

The actual places for Carmelite living may be quite varied, but a preference for the poor must be a continual option. The option of the Filipina, Aram, is to live and work among the truly poor and marginalized. She hears the tradition in this context of material and political poverty.

Unable to be involved in direct ministry, Thérèse of Lisieux was driven to the heart of the matter. She realized that all ministry, all true service of the world had to be based on love. She could do nothing heroic or grand for the world, but she could live her confined life with a great love. Reading St. Paul assured her that love was a "more excellent way."[16] She would be love in the heart of the church. Her martyrdom for the world would be an emptying of herself, a submission to God's love, a self-abandonment with total confidence in the mercy of God. Her very inability to concretely aid others seemed to intensify her longing. A biographer captured her desires:

> Thérèse knew that, sitting in her cell with her small writing-desk on her lap, she was writing foolish things. She was no longer satisfied with her vocation to be a Carmelite, a spouse, a mother....she would like to be a *warrior, a priest, a deacon, an apostle, a doctor of the Church, a martyr.* And she wanted to experience each of these vocations in all its fullness, in space and time. To preach the Gospel in the five continents of the world, to be a missionary from the dawn of creation till the end of time, to be martyred in every possible way; these desires which tortured her were *greater than the universe.* [17]

The "place" of the Carmelite friar, Titus Brandsma, was in Holland during the Nazi occupation. His was an academic life, but he was also champion of Catholic education and the Dutch Catholic press. Nazi decrees threatened the control and the very existence of the schools and the press. Titus traveled throughout Holland on behalf of the church, meeting with editors and journalists encouraging them to resist Nazi control. He wrote a letter on behalf of the bishops to all the editors of Catholic papers. He realized the danger associated with being in this "place": "We are not sure yet if those responsible will resort to violence. But in case they do, remember, God speaks the last word and He rewards His faithful servant."[18]

His service of those whose rights were denied led him to the concentration camps. His words about his prison cell at Scheveningen help us realize that the essence of the tradition is an attentiveness to a God who is ever faithful:

> "Beata solitudo, blessed solitude." I am already quite at home in this small cell. I have not yet got bored here, just the contrary. I am alone, certainly, but never was Our Lord so near to me. I could shout for joy because he made me find him again entirely, without me being able to go to see people, nor people me. Now he is my only refuge, and I feel secure and happy. I would stay here for ever, if he so disposed. Seldom have I been so happy and content.[19]

The mendicant has been constricted to his hermitage where it all began, and there he finds the Presence who had accompanied and vivified his ministry.

Titus was steeped in the Carmelite tradition. He taught and wrote about its spirituality. For nineteen years he had lectured at the Catholic University of Nijmegen, which he helped found. The positions he took on behalf of justice flowed naturally from his contemplative life. For his service in the midst of the people Titus was martyred at Dachau on July 26, 1942.

"We Poor"

Contemplative prayer naturally issues in concern for social justice. If prayer is authentic, a true listening and wording, then one is led into our common humanity, into the reality of the human condition. At that point there are no rich and poor, privileged and underprivileged. What is revealed is fragile, sinful, blessed humanity.

We admit we cannot guarantee our loves; we cannot safeguard our lives; we are not our own cause and creator. We enter into a poverty of spirit and wait on God's mercy. This condition is the deepest source of solidarity with the world. We have to wait in hope with all who wait in hope. We can truly say, "We poor."

Thérèse of Lisieux learned her essential poverty in a cloistered convent in France. She read in her sister's notebook a passage from scripture, "Whoever is a little one, let him come to me" (Prv 9:4). She let go of any heroic ideal and realized that littleness was her way.

"And for this," she wrote, "I had no need to grow up, but rather I had to remain *little* and become this more and more."[20] Thérèse's poverty of spirit threw her on the mercy of God. It is telling to realize the millions of people who feel an affinity with this "little flower." In her "little way" she touched the hearts of all who feel little in life. She gave them hope in their littleness and assured them that littleness was enough. This young woman had distilled the prescriptions of the Rule given to the men on Mount Carmel, and the teachings of the great Carmelite mystics whom she admired, into an expression easily understood by countless readers. They saw in her one of their own, a little one, a poor one.[21]

First Response: Gratitude and Song

The foundation for the work of justice and peace is the unmerited love of God, given us freely. The gratuitousness of this love is the overwhelming reality of our lives, more overwhelming than even the direst analysis of the poverty of our world. The wellspring of our activity and ministry with the poor is not our sympathetic analysis, but the realization of the mercy of God who forgives, heals, strengthens, and brings life. This uncontrollable, incomprehensible Mystery is seen most vividly in the life and teachings of Jesus, but most especially in his passion and cross. God so loved us that God gave his son. And the son so loved the father than he continued to trust that love even in the heart of the darkness on the cross.

So, the first word of justice and peace is not prophetic denunciation, condemnation, or grief. The first word is a word of *gratitude*, of thanksgiving, of joy. Its proper expression is in the heart that dances and sings. Elijah, in the mythical story of the *Institution of the First Monks* indoctrinated his followers into prophecy, which for them meant the activity of *singing God's praises accompanied by musical instruments*.[22] In gratitude and song they announced the presence and faithfulness of God who saves the people.

One proceeds to the work of justice not from a position of anger, nor from guilt, nor from a sense of fairness, nor from a sympathetic heart, and not because the poor are better. We minister with the poor because God has chosen to live with us and wants all to participate in the gifts of creation, and be happy with God forever. Where people are not able to participate in these gifts, the presence of God is most clearly seen. God's will is most evident here, and in that way we can say that God resides with the poor. Our work of justice is a response to this love. It becomes God's work, God's way of inviting all to the banquet of life.

Second Response: A Word of Justice

The realization of the mercy of God situates justice within the context of God's gratuitous love. The language of prophetic grieving and denunciation is buoyed on the language of contemplation and worship. In actual lives the two languages may be quite separate, one language perhaps being foreign. But, ideally, the two languages may become one language. It is the language of song and deliverance. Gustavo Gutiérrez writes: "Mystical language expresses the gratuitousness of God's love, prophetic language expresses the demands this love makes."[23]

A language begun in denunciation and prophetic activity may learn, from the communities of the impoverished, how to give thanks to God even in the midst of deprivation. As Carmel teaches, God's gratuitous, freeing love may be first met in the exhaustion and darkness of our feeble efforts. In the dark we learn to lay down our own arms, put on the armor of faith, and return to battle with renewed strength. We return thankful and singing, and then the work of justice flows naturally like water from the temple.

The Witness of a Prayerful Community

From the beginning of this tradition in Palestine, life with others has been an integral component of Carmelite spirituality. Time has only strengthened the value of living as a community. Every reform worked to shore up the foundations of community life.

As elementary as living together and praying together seems, the witness of such a community can be one of the most powerful actions on behalf of a more just and peaceful world. In a world rent with divisions, people living peacefully together cannot be underestimated. Built into the Rule of Carmel is a prescription for the first Carmelites to come together each week and discuss their difficulties with one another. Forces within individuals and between individuals continually splinter efforts at cohesion.

A vital community life lived in friendship and equality gives witness to the possibility of a world where men and women can live in harmony. If this community can share its gifts and resources, and live simply, it makes attractive the possibility of alternate forms of living not based on power, money, or prestige.

Teresa of Avila said that the best text for her sisters to read was the text of their relationships with one another. Remember her ideals: "All must be friends, all must be loved, all must be held dear, all must be helped."[24] If they could read how well they were doing in making real these ideals, they would know how authentic their prayer was.

Tens of thousands of men and women have made their religious life vows according to the Carmelite Rule. Many thousands of others have associated with Carmel and follow Carmel's Rule modified for their situations in life.[25] Countless others simply draw from this tradition whatever is helpful to them in their lives. Most of these men and women attempt to lead lives accountable to others in small faith communities. The small band of hermits who began the Carmelite tradition have, today, a living legacy.

The Generals of the two Carmelite orders have urged such a witness for today's world:

> We are talking about community which is born out of listening to the Word of God, and so humanises its members, brings people together despite their differences and is thus a true presence of the Gospel. In this way our communities will become signs of hope which will cause the poor to say about us what the widow of Zarepta said about Elijah, "Now I know that you are truly a man of God and that the word of the Lord in your mouth is truth" (1 Kgs 17:24).[26]

A prayerful community, living simply, cannot help but produce life around it. It will live in a way which is peaceful and just and liberating, and in its ministry these qualities will be evident.[27] The Carmelite tradition brings to the struggle a simple, but powerful resource: a prayerful community of friends.

Elijah, Once More

Today Carmelites are looking at the fiery prophet Elijah once again.[28] They began on his mountain and saw in him a model of their life. Like Elijah they were to live a life of detachment and purity of heart, and open their minds and hearts to the experience of God. Today, Carmelites are remembering Elijah's criticism of the status quo which was an unfair situation for so many. We are recalling that he challenged the powers in control, both civil and religious establishments. He dueled the idols which had usurped the true God's place in the lives of the people. As did his follower Eliseus, all who thirst for justice ask for a portion of his spirit, his zeal, his sense of mission.

The martyrs of our day, people who gave of their lives for others because they identified with the persecuted in their following of Christ, have called us all to a reexamination of our lives. Within the Carmelite family, the deaths of Titus Brandsma and Edith Stein[29] have been a recent reminder of the demonic loose in the world, and the serious implications of "living in allegiance to Jesus Christ." The issue is being joined in urban areas, barrios, ghettos, on borders, in war-torn areas, among immigrants, with the young and the defenceless.

Leadership within the Carmelites has asked its membership to be open to entering the world "where the night is darkest, especially among the poor and marginalized, since it is there that God has made himself more present and that his presence can be discovered in new ways. It is there that, like Elijah, we can sense the gentle breeze (1 Kgs 19:12)."[30]

The scene in the cell of Titus Brandsma is a poignant, yet powerfully faith-filled, summary of the tradition he taught and loved. Imprisoned for his prophetic denunciation of Nazi attempts to control the Dutch Catholic press, the friar constructed an "altar":

> There has to be something appealing in such a bare cell! Before me I have a small altar, or whatever you may like to call it. I found a paper checkerboard in my cell with checkers. I don't think I shall start playing, but I also found a piece of packing paper. I wrapped it around the board and, using a nail from a cigar box—one has to manage to get on, for I have been deprived of both knife and scissors—I made three nicks in the packing paper; in these nicks I put three holy pictures from my breviary.
>
> So in front of me I have the picture of Christ on the Cross, and although it is not full length, at least it is a nice bust with the wound of the Sacred Heart, and it is Fra Angelico, too! On one side of it I put St. Teresa with her motto: "To die or to suffer," and on the other side St. John of the Cross with his: "To suffer and to be contemned." I also found two pins and I used one for putting under the three pictures a paper with St. Teresa's motto, "Nada te turbe, etc." in the middle: "Gott so nah und ferne, Gott ist immer da;" and lastly my favourite maxim: "Prenez les jours comme ils arrivent."
>
> I had no stray picture of Our Lady in my breviary—and surely her image ought to be in a Carmelite's cell. I managed this too. In the part of the breviary we are using now, and which was luckily left to me, is the beautiful picture of Our Lady of Mount Carmel. So now my breviary is standing wide open on the topmost of the two corner shelves, to the left of the bed. When sitting at my table I only have to look a bit to the right and I can see her beautiful picture; while lying in bed my eye is firstly caught by that star-bearing Madonna, Hope of all Carmelites.[31]

NOTES

1. In their document, "Justice in the World," a Synod of Bishops in 1971 made this challenging statement: "Action on behalf of justice and participation in the transformation of the world fully appear to us as a constitutive dimension of the preaching of the Gospel, or, in other words, of the Church's mission for the redemption of the human race and its liberation from every oppressive situation." *The Gospel of Peace and Justice,* presented by Joseph Gremillion (Maryknoll, New York: Orbis Books, 1976), 514.

2. Pope Paul VI defined evangelization in this manner: "For the Church, evangelizing means bringing the Good News into all strata of humanity, and through its influence transforming humanity from within and making it new...The Church evangelizes when she seeks to convert, solely through the divine power of the message she proclaims, both the personal and collective consciences of people, the activities in which they engage, and the lives and concrete milieu which are theirs." *On Evangelization in the Modern World,* #18.

3. Araceli (Aram) Carcellar, "Carmelite Identity from the Perspective of the Rule: A Lay Experience," in *The Carmelite Family* (Melbourne: Carmelite Communications, 1994), 56.

4. *The Institution of the First Monks*, trans. Norman Werling, O. Carm., in *The Sword,* 5 (1941), 243. Peace, the *shalom* of God, is a free gift, effecting a reconciliation between humankind and God, as well as a reconciliation among peoples, and within individuals. Christ's church has a mission of reconciliation in the world. Latin American bishops at Medellin taught that peace is a work of justice. It presupposes a just order in which people have dignity, the satisfaction of legitimate aspirations, access to truth, and freedom.

5. *The Carmelite Family,* 55, 56.

6. John of the Cross, "The Spiritual Canticle," in *The Collected Works of St. John of the Cross,* trans. Kieran Kavanaugh, O.C.D., and Otilio Rodriguez, O.C.D. (Washington, D.C.: ICS Publications, 1991), stanza 7.

7. *The Carmelite Family,* 57.

8. Segundo Galilea, *The Future of Our Past* (Notre Dame, Indiana: Ave Maria Press, 1985), 55.

9. Teresa of Avila, "A Satirical Critique," in *The Collected Works of St. Teresa of Avila,* 3, trans. Kieran Kavanaugh, O.C.D., and Otilio Rodriguez, O.C.D. (Washington, D.C.: ICS Publications, 1985), 360, 361.

10. *The Carmelite Family,* 57, 58.

11. One general assessment of the mendicants states: "But much

had been achieved through the ministry of the friars. The urban poor as well as the rural peasantry had the Gospel preached to them. The clergy as well as the people had been offered religious instruction. The devout life, hitherto regarded as the exclusive occupation of clergy and enclosed religious, had been made available to the laity. The enthusiasm for the Apostolic Life had been channeled into new religious institutes and had been largely contained within the Church. Heresy had retreated before the well-equipped forces of militant orthodoxy. The Mendicant schoolmen had given fresh life and a new orientation to Western theology and philosophy. Through their efforts, the intellectual crisis precipitated by the reception of pagan philosophy and science into the schools had terminated in a Christian synthesis." C.H. Lawrence, *The Friars* (London and New York: Longman, 1994), 227, 228.

12. "The missionary enterprise was the *raison d'être* of the Mendicant Orders....Many of their men were accustomed to leaving their own country for the sake of learning, teaching or administration." Ibid., 202. The Master General of the Dominicans, in 1255, complained of two things which hindered missionary work: the "lack of languages" and the "love of one's native soil, a natural affection not yet transformed by grace." Ibid.

13. In a recent letter to the Carmelite and Discalced Carmelite Orders, the two Generals wrote: "We acknowledge that the past is still part of us, and we feel close to those brothers and sisters who have gone before us, in their carmelite and pastoral life, in good times and in bad.

"Thus, while we thank God for the lives they led and for their making the Kingdom present, we also ask forgiveness, in their name, of both the indigenous and the afroamerican peoples for the mistakes and shortcomings in the process of evangelisation." *A Praying Community at the Service of the People* (Rome, 1992), pars. 8, 9.

14. Cf. Carlos Mesters, O. Carm., "The Carmelite Mystical Tradition at the Service of the Poor," in *Liberation Spirituality: Carmelite Perspectives.,* ed. by David Blanchard, O. Carm., in *Sword,* vol. 47 (1987).

15. John of the Cross, "The Spiritual Canticle," in *The Collected Works*, Canticle A, stanza 35.

16. 1 Cor. 12:31.

17. Guy Gaucher, *The Story of a Life: St. Thérèse of Lisieux,* trans. Sr. Anne Marie Brennan, ODC (San Francisco: HarperSanFrancisco, 1987), 169.

18. *Essays on Titus Brandsma*, ed. Redemptus Valabek, O. Carm. (Rome: Carmel in the World Paperbacks, 1985), 26.

19. Ibid., 295.

20. Thérèse of Lisieux, *Story of a Soul*, trans. John Clarke, O.C.D. (Washington, D.C.: ICS Publications, 1976), 208.

21. The Latin American bishops at Medellin related spiritual childhood and solidarity with the poor of the world. A poor Church, they wrote, "denounces the unjust lack of this world's goods and the sin that begets it; preaches and lives in spiritual poverty, as an attitude of spiritual childhood and openness to the Lord; is herself bound to material poverty. The poverty of the Church is, in effect, a constant factor in the history of salvation." *The Gospel of Peace and Justice*, 473.

22. *The Institution of the First Monks*, 5 (1941), 21.

23. Gustavo Gutiérrez, *On Job*, trans. Matthew J. O'Connell (Quezon City, Philippines: Claretian Publications, 1987), 95.

24. Teresa of Avila, *The Way of Perfection*, in *The Collected Works of St. Teresa of Avila*, 2, chap. 4, no. 7.

25. For example, in the United States there are approximately 14,000 "lay" or "secular" Carmelites who meet regularly in small communities to pray, to reflect on their lives in the light of scripture, to support one another, and to draw from the Carmelite tradition resources for living a life in "allegiance to Jesus Christ."

26. *A Praying Community at the Service of the People*, par. 25.

27. Teresa of Avila saw a necessary connection between prayer and service: "I repeat, it is necessary that your foundation consist of more than prayer and contemplation....Let us desire and be occupied in prayer not for the sake of our enjoyment but so as to have this strength to serve....Believe me, Martha and Mary must join together...." *The Interior Castle*, in *The Collected Works*, 2, The Seventh Dwelling Places, chap. 4, nos. 9 and 12.

28. Cf. Mesters.

29. Edith Stein (1891–1942) was a Jewish convert to Catholicism who later became a Carmelite nun, Sr. Teresa Benedict of the Cross. As a young woman, and an acknowledged atheist, she had been a distinguished student of philosophy, mentored by Edmund Husserl, the father of phenomenology.

The autobiography of St. Teresa of Avila was influential in Edith's decision to become a Catholic. Edith was an educator and an early writer on women's issues. At the age of forty-two she entered the Carmel of Cologne. Edith related her entry into Carmel to the need to pray for the coming persecution of her Jewish people. She moved to the Carmel in Echt, Holland, for greater safety. Her sister Rosa, now baptized, joined her in Echt and served as the portress. However, the Nazis began arresting Catholics of Jewish descent, and the two sisters were taken from their

Carmel. Edith and Rosa were eventually transported to Auschwitz where they were murdered on August 9, 1942. Two weeks earlier, Titus Brandsma had been killed at Dachau.

30. *A Praying Community at the Service of the People*, par. 22.

31. *Essays on Titus Brandsma,* 294.

Chapter Ten

DESIRING WHAT GOD DESIRES

The Divinization of Our Humanity

The language of the Carmelites is often bold. When John of the Cross describes the outcome of a contemplative life, he speaks of a transformation so profound that *we become God.* For John, the attentive listening for God's presence and activity in one's life, and a willingness to be transformed by that love, results in divinization.[1]

John describes the goal of the Christian journey in particularly lyrical terms in *The Living Flame of Love,* both the poem and the commentary. There he searches for words for his experience of a union with God so transforming that he characterizes it as divinization, or deification. He describes an intensely personal, intimate love relationship between the soul and God, a profound union in the very core of his being.

At times, in reading John of the Cross with his language of *nada,* stillness, and solitude, one might assume that the contemplative is becoming more and more withdrawn and ends up in isolation. This assumption fits in well with a stereotypical look often associated with a saintly or holy person. One writer described it this way: you knew a person was holy when he held his head at ten after six, and looked as if he had just received bad news the rest of us had not yet heard.

But what is truly happening when we "become God"? It is helpful to review John's analysis of human desire. He observed that the desires of the heart are restless, pulling us now here, now there. They are like little children calling for attention, and will not be still for very long. He noticed that even when the heart achieved something it deeply desired, it was satisfied for only a while, and then desires once more began tugging at the heart. John likened the condition to the situation of a lover who eagerly anticipates a special day with the beloved, and it turns out to be a deep disappointment. John concluded that we humans have a yearning, a hunger, for which only God is sufficient food. Any other nourishment which promises complete satisfaction distorts our life.

But, as the heart gropingly reaches out for a God it often cannot name, the heart continually gives itself away to what is not God. In seeking the fulfillment of its desires our heart continually asks other people, projects, situations, plans, communities to be its God, to be fulfillment of its deepest desires. The heart asks a part of God's creation to be ultimate, to be God. The heart creates idols, and in giving itself to these idols, in centering its life around them as though they were God, the heart becomes enslaved. These are attachments, in John's language, but he also says the condition is one of an enslaved heart. In giving itself so fully to its attachments, its idols, the heart is no longer free to respond to the invitation from the gracious presence at the center.

John of the Cross urges an ascetical freeing of the heart. But in his own situation he reports that he could not loosen his grasp of that to which he was clinging for dear life. Teresa of Avila reported the same problem. The more she tried to detach from her idols, to de-center herself from false centers, the more she was enmeshed.

John learned that only God's love could entice him from his idols. Right where his desires were exhausting themselves trying to find fulfillment, in the dark of his apparent failure, John experienced a kindling of a deeper love. This love invited him past his deteriorating situation; it reordered his other loves; and it allowed him to slowly relax his grasp on his life and trustingly renew life's journey.

Going Deeper in God

Using an image similar to Teresa's pilgrimage to the interior of the castle, John describes the spiritual journey as a journey to the center where God dwells. "The soul's center is God," he writes. But this center is not a distant center to be reached after a lifetime of effort. No, John says whoever has even one degree of love is in the center, is in God. It is a matter of degrees. With each degree of love the soul travels more deeply into its center, or as John writes about the soul: "Although it is in its center, it is not yet in its deepest center, for it can go *deeper in God*."[2]

This going deeper in God is a divinizing process. John writes, "...once it has attained the final degree, God's love has arrived at wounding the soul in its ultimate and deepest center, which is to illuminate and transform it in its whole being, power, and strength, and according to its capacity, *until it appears to be God*."[3]

John reports a remarkable transformation of his heart's desire as a result of going deeper in God. His desire and God's desire have now joined in a consonance of desires. He reports to God:

> What you desire me to ask for, I ask for; and what you do not desire, I do not desire, nor can I, nor does it even enter my mind to desire it. My petitions are now more valuable and estimable in your sight, since they come from You, and You move me to make them, and I make them in the delight and joy of the Holy Spirit, *my judgment now issuing from Your countenance* [Ps 17:2], that is, when You esteem and hear my prayer.[4]

In this process he says that faith is stretching our intellect toward God beyond any created thing; and hope is freeing our memory from past recollections as well as future scenarios, allowing us to live in pure expectancy; and our will more and more is loving with God's love.

> Accordingly, the intellect of this soul is God's intellect; its will is God's will; its memory is the memory of God; and its delight is God's delight; and although the substance of this soul is not the substance of God, since it cannot undergo a substantial conversion into Him, *it has become God through participation in God*, being

> united to and absorbed in Him, as it is in this state....the soul can well repeat the words of St. Paul: "I live, now not I, but Christ lives in me."[5]

John continues to attempt to word the experience of divinization: "This is the soul's deep satisfaction and happiness: To see that it gives God more than it is worth in itself, the very divine light and divine heat that are given to it."[6]

In writing about the intense moments within the experience of union with God in *The Living Flame of Love* John says, "Thus in this state the soul cannot make acts because *the Holy Spirit makes them all* and moves it toward them. As a result all the acts of the soul are divine....the activity of God in God."[7]

Again, "This feast takes place in the substance of the soul....*Thus all the movements of this soul are divine.* Although they belong to it, they belong to it because God works them in it and with it, for it wills and consents to them."[8]

Loving with God's Love

John charts the purification of desire through the dark nights of sense and spirit. He seems to be saying that when we love on the merely sense level we love in a disordered way which turns everything back toward us and our immediate fulfillment. We love in a way which seeks our happiness, our gratification. Through the night of the senses, an order is brought into our appetites and our manner of living. The sense faculties and the spiritual faculties are now in harmony, and we love in a more thoughtful and responsible manner.

Now we do not love simply because the object of our love satisfies us. Now we love because we deliberately choose to love. We love because we understand we should love. We love the other because, apart from what we think about them or what we receive back from our love, God has given them immense worth and dignity and we love them as God's creation, a brother or sister. There may be no immediate pleasure or satisfaction, but we choose to love anyway because it is the right thing to do. We may even choose to love our enemy, as Jesus taught. Our love now seems properly ordered and directed, and our life is a gospel-oriented life.

But John seems to report an even further transformation. Through the experiences which he called the night of the spirit, in which his spiritual faculties of intellect, memory, and will were purified even more, the intention for our love seems to pass from us and go into God. We no longer, essentially, have the reason for our love. The intention, the motivation for our love is now in God, and all we can do is love.

The person and God are so united, and there is such a consonance of desires, it is as though God were loving God in our love, as though God were loving God's world in our love, and all we can do is live in the world in a way which is loving. And the reason essentially is no longer in us. John writes: "...the soul here loves God, not through itself, but through him."[9] Our life has taken on a Trinitarian form. Christ's spirit is in us loving the creator and all creation.

We have here a remarkable testimony to the potential of our humanity. Perhaps this is why Evelyn Underhill calls the mystics "pioneers of humanity." They have been to places in their humanity which beckon in all of us.

Living without a Why

Meister Eckhart has a challenging observation regarding the total detachment seen in John's divinized person. Eckhart, a fourteenth-century Dominican, spoke of detachment as the greatest of virtues. The ultimate detachment for Eckhart would be to learn to "live without a why." Eckhart speaks of an inner place, similar to John's substance of the soul, where "God's ground is my ground, and my ground is God's ground....It is out of this inner ground that you should perform all your works without asking, 'Why?'"[10]

Eckhart further describes his radical sense of detachment:

> So long as you perform your works for the sake of the kingdom of heaven, or for God's sake, or for the sake

> of your eternal blessedness, and you work them from without, you are going completely astray....Whoever is seeking God by "ways" is finding "ways" and losing God, who in ways is hidden. But whoever seeks for God without ways will find him as he is in himself, and that man will live with the Son, and he is life itself.
>
> If anyone went on for a thousand years asking of life: "Why are you living?" Life if it could answer, would only say: 'I live so that I may live.' That is because life lives out of its own ground and springs from its own source, and so it lives without asking why it is itself living.
>
> If anyone asked a truthful man who works out of his own ground "Why are you performing your works?" and if he were to give a straight answer, he would only say, "I work so that I may work."[11]

Is this detached, divinized person an automaton? Does this person no longer have to reflect and make decisions because the Holy Spirit has taken over? It certainly does not appear that John became robotic. His intellect still functioned, but now divinely, and so also with his memory and will. The union with God seems to intimate that the person is functioning in a beautifully human way and that human way of functioning, of knowing and loving, is now in total accord with God's will, with God's knowing and loving this world.

Now, apparently, the way the person understands this world and its interrelationships is in accord with God's view, and what and how the person loves is now in accord with God's love. The faculties all need to continue to function but they result in a human life which naturally cooperates with God's kingdom. This person is now living in a way which is in accord with God's will, which is the well-being of humanity. The way this person lives now furthers a world of love, of justice, of peace. The many "words" of this person now say the one Word who is God.

Are there many people who live in this condition of divinization? How many people really do live without a "why"? Eckhart warns that such people are hard to identify.

> But note, you must pay heed, for such people are very hard to recognize. When others fast, they eat, when others watch, they sleep, when others pray, they are silent—in short, all their words and acts are unknown to other people; because whatever good people practice while on their way to eternal bliss, all that is quite foreign to such perfected ones. They need absolutely nothing, for they are in possession of the city of their true birthright.[12]

Their contemplation of God is habitual and overflows in works of love.

Now, many of us fit this description. When others are fasting we are eating, when they watch in vigil we are asleep, and when they pray we are silent. Obviously, some other criteria must be used to differentiate those who are living without a why from those of us who are living without a clue.

Teresa's Transformation

Teresa of Avila provided one of the more detailed descriptions of this state of intimate union with God, the condition John calls divinization. In discussing her situation in the seventh dwelling place in *The Interior Castle*, the situation of the mystical marriage, Teresa describes the changes in herself.

Teresa reports a close union with God, but God does not preoccupy her. As a matter of fact, because of this union in the "extreme interior" she said she was more fully engaged in her ministry than ever before. And when she turned her attention to God, God was right there. While enjoying this intimate union with God, Teresa is deeply involved in all the practical tasks of founding new communities in her reform.

Teresa also reports that she could, finally, simply forget herself. She learned that if she would take care of the things of God, God would take care of the things of Teresa. One of the greatest realizations in her life had been that God desired her. When she was able to accept the fact that God desired her, she was freed from the need to continually ask others, in one form or another, if she were desirable.

Teresa still had a great desire to suffer, but the desire was not troubling as before. She writes: "For the desire left in these souls that the will of God be done in them reaches such an extreme that they think everything His Majesty does is good. If He desires the soul to suffer, well and good; if not it doesn't kill itself as it used to."[13] Because she is more in tune with God, Teresa mistrusts herself less. When she was living mainly on the periphery of the castle, her life fragmented in many centers, she could not trust her desires. By the time she reports the experiences of the seventh dwelling place she now "wants what God wants" and is less suspicious of herself.

As a matter of fact, Teresa reports being free of even the desire to die and complete her pilgrimage. In the sixth dwelling place there was great suffering because she was aware of her sinfulness and her distance from God, as well as her immense unfulfilled desires. She wanted to finish the journey and complete her union with God. Now, however, in the seventh dwelling place it is no longer a matter of what *she* wants. She said she no longer desires to die, but desires to live and for many years if God would be served. If God wants her to stay and serve, she stays for however long God wants. If God calls her home, she goes gladly. She is free now and wants only what God wants. She always taught, the purpose of prayer is conformity with God's will. "Few there are," she writes, "who, detached from everything else, really look after His honor."[14]

Now she reports a deep interior joy when persecuted, without hostility or evil wishes for her persecutors. As a matter of fact, she has great compassion on them and would help them if they needed her.

She said that now she wants either to be alone, or to be serving souls. The great paradox, and tension, of being a solitary in community seems to have found a resolution in her. She is living from a place where the two are fundamentally one.

She no longer experiences dryness in prayer, nor does she have ecstatic experiences. (Only occasionally, she admits, but rarely in public). Apparently her visions and voices, and other extraordinary experiences, were the result of her humanity being amplified and accommodated to the divine. Much like a space ship, she eventually settled into the atmosphere of her new milieu, a divine milieu.

She concludes by warning her nuns not to build castles in the air. This loving condition they are in manifests itself in concrete care for the ones with whom one lives, and in the appropriate situations of one's possibilities in life.

The Divinized Person

After hearing John's description of his experience of being divinized, of his desire being honed, and after listening to Teresa's descriptions of her transformation, what can be said about the divinized person? What does he or she look like?

The divinized person seems to be one who is truly *alive*, whose powers have been brought to life, actuated. The person will not have abilities she did not previously have, but she will be free to use the gifts she has received.

The whole personality has been brought into harmony with its center. It no longer wars against itself, or operates in a dysfunctional way. She is *integrated.*

There is a self-possession which is so profound that it allows a giving of self, a *self-transcendence.*

The divinized person is grounded or *rooted* in a graciousness at the core of the personality. Her life naturally manifests acceptance, compassion, generosity, and humility. Others are esteemed, and community grows.

Because the person is knowing this world with God's knowing, and loving it with God's loving, she can love this world, be committed to it, be passionate about it, without clutching, grabbing, without the heart being fragmented or enslaved, and without distorting the world. In other words, this person loves with a *freedom of heart, a freedom of spirit.* She is free to be the creation God meant her to be and free to love the world as it truly is and for its good.

Are there many people like this? Well, remembering Eckhart's warning that they are hard to identify, I still think we would have to say there are many people in this condition. John of the Cross said that even with one degree of love a person is in the center, but there are other centers and one can go deeper in God. I take it to mean that this divinization is a process, a journey with many stages, always a pilgrimage, but a graced pilgrimage. The center has come to us.

Maybe the flame of our spirit and the flame of God's spirit are not one flame yet, but in their dance they touch one another, and go apart, they flicker within one another, they sometimes are lost within one another. John encourages us to open ourselves to this dance that the flames may be one.

Each soul is learning to tell the story of being human—that is, a story of being pursued into life and freedom by a love which is at our core and fuels our journey. John of the Cross says that we are becoming God through participation in God, and he invites us to give ourselves over to the flame without fear, but with patience, perseverance, and gratitude.

NOTES

1. Early Greek theologians, particularly, developed the theme of divinization, a participation in God's life in union with Christ. John of the Cross stresses that the creature always remains a creature, and never becomes uncreated.

2. John of the Cross, *The Living Flame of Love*, in *The Collected Works of St. John of the Cross*, trans. Kieran Kavanaugh, O.C.D., and Otilio Rodriguez, O.C.D. (Washington, D.C.: ICS Publications, 1991), stanza 1, no. 12.

3. Ibid., no. 13.

4. Ibid., no. 36.

5. Ibid., stanza 2, no. 34.

6. Ibid., stanza 3, no. 80.

7. Ibid., stanza 1, no. 4.

8. Ibid., no. 9.

9. Ibid., stanza 3, no. 82.

10. Edmund Colledge, O.S.A., and Bernard McGinn, trans. and intro., *Meister Eckhart* (New York: Paulist Press, 1981), 183.

11. Ibid., 183, 184.

12. Richard Woods, O.P., *Eckhart's Way* (Wilmington, Delaware: Michael Glazier, 1986), 146, 147.

13. Teresa of Avila, *The Interior Castle* in *The Collected Works of St. Teresa of Avila*, 2, trans. Kieran Kavanaugh, O.C.D., and Otilio Rodriguez, O.C.D. (Washington, D.C.: ICS Publications, 1980), The Seventh Dwelling Places, chap. 3, no. 4.

14. Ibid., no. 6.

Epilogue

The Rule of Carmel encourages an attentive listening for God's presence and activity in one's life, and a willingness to be transformed by that love. The original setting of the Carmelites was in a canyon on a mountain ridge. There, ruminating on God's word in scripture, the Carmelite was led into an inner land, an interior desert, where God pursues the soul into life. It is a story happening in every human life. The Carmelites have learned to tell the story in their own unique language.

When asked who they were, Carmelites said they were people from a mountain on whose heights and in whose valleys men and women gathered to worship God. They eventually left the mountain, but it continued to provide the atmosphere within which later Carmelite life was lived. Its memory, and the stories told there, continued to haunt the community.

When Carmelites forgot their roots and began to live other stories with other values, people like Nicholas the Frenchman, through his letter known in the order as *The Flaming Arrow*, reminded them of the purpose of their life on Mount Carmel. He resigned as General of the Order in discouragement. Nicholas probably had good reason to be concerned about the direction of the order, but he perhaps underestimated the resiliency of the tradition. Carmel was able to find authentic expression in conditions different from its origins.

As imperfectly as their life may have been lived in the new mendicant conditions in Europe in the 1200s, Carmelites, nonetheless, effectively responded to the call of the church and the needs of the people. A prayerful life, lived in community, and generously serving others, has remained a constant Carmelite ideal. It continues to be expressed in a variety of lifestyles.

In the first two centuries of the order's existence the figures of Mary and Elijah arose as icons with particular significance for Carmelites. Philip Ribot's late-fourteenth-century *The Institution of the First Monks* wove a story which identified Elijah and Mary as foundational figures in the order's self-understanding. They were raised up as individuals who preeminently exemplified the ascetical and mystical tradition of Carmel. Their hearts were free for God, unencumbered with idolatrous pursuits. The order became known as a Marian order, inspired by Elijah's zeal for God. The Carmelite was told to expect to experience God in mind and heart.

The original vision continued through the centuries, sometimes lived heroically, at other times less so. Periodically, individuals arose calling for renewal. They reminded the order of the first community on the mountain, the Rule, Elijah, Mary, and the vision they evoked. The clearest and most effective call to renew the vision came from Teresa of Avila in sixteenth-century Spain. Joined by John of the Cross, Teresa challenged Carmelites to live within the tension of being hermits in community, solitaries who lived a common life with brothers and sisters, at the service of the church. She taught the absolute necessity of a prayer which listened for God's approach and invited inner transformation.

Teresa and John illumined the soul, throwing light on its illusions. They helped us realize how we can take something good and make it a god, thereby distorting the good, neglecting God, and further diminishing our humanity. In the primordial language of their images and poetry, and through their prose expositions, they identified a healing process which God's love initiates. By urging cooperation with that transforming love, they pointed the way to purity of heart, a freedom of spirit. They encouraged us to stand our ground in trust when God's love is dark, believing that in those times we are being purified and invited into a deeper union.

Teresa and John taught us the potential of our humanity, and the flowering of our baptismal promises. An openness to God's spirit at work in our lives can lead to a transformation of our desires. Eventually our desires are less and less fragmenting, and more and more we desire what God desires, in a consonance of desire. If we may say that God desires the well-being of humanity, then this transformed person now lives in a way which promotes that well-being, especially where people obviously are deprived of their rightful places at the banquet of life.

Teresa's reform eventually became an order itself, the Discalced Carmelites. The Teresian reform greatly influenced the Reform of Touraine which helped inspire renewal throughout the original Carmelite Order. Touraine numbered among its members John of St.-Samson, the blind "mystic" of Rennes, who became the unofficial spiritual director for generations of novices and professed students. The reform acknowledged the church's call to active ministry and study, but emphasized that, for Carmelites, contemplation was still "the principal part."

Today, Carmelites are more deeply aware that contemplative prayer should issue in solidarity with all who have to wait in hope for God's mercy. Contemplative prayer should be the deepest source of compassion for our suffering world. Such openness to God's love and its fire, results in a poverty of spirit, a restoration of reverence, and a sensitivity to the plight of our brothers and sisters.

Our first response to the overwhelming experience of God's freely-given love is gratitude. Elijah taught the community on Mount Carmel the prophecy of praising God accompanied by musical instruments.

Thérèse of Lisieux found St. Paul's words to the Romans to be true in her life: "So it depends not on human will or exertion, but on God who shows mercy" (9:16). Her "little way" is an acknowledgment that this love cannot be earned, won, or bought. It is offered, free. Before we know it or can do anything about it, we are loved, desired, accepted. Thérèse and all others in this tradition who have let this love reveal itself sing this conviction. Eventually, we have to learn to let go, and trust. "It is all grace!" she concluded.

Teresa of Avila came to the same conclusion. Our lives are a story, ultimately, not of our failures or triumphs, but of God's mercies. That is the true story of our lives. When we learn to tell it right, then we are entering more fully into the truth of our existence.

The second response to God's freely given love is the prophetic word which grieves for those not able to partake of the banquet of life. This word is the word that points out injustice and cries for redress.

Here, too, Elijah has become a significant figure in our day, as one who cried out and took the side of the poor and oppressed. He defended God's honor against the idols of the day. Carmelites are recovering the social justice exigency natural to the tradition. Titus Brandsma and Edith Stein have exemplified such prophetic impulses.

Albert, Carmel's rule-giver, ended the Rule saying: "Here then are a few points I have written down to provide you with a standard of conduct to live up to; *but our Lord, at his Second Coming will reward anyone who does more than he is obliged to do*." A modern commentator makes a challenging point: in this probable allusion to the parable of the Good Samaritan, the Carmelite is cast in the role of the innkeeper. A stranger brings him a person who has been found beaten and abandoned on the side of the road. The stranger orders the innkeeper to take care of this wounded person, and do whatever else might be necessary. On his return, the stranger will repay the innkeeper for any additional expenses.

The innkeeper, the Carmelite, has had the order and control of his house upset by a visitor, the Messiah. He is asked to bind the wounds of the Messiah's people in his absence. The innkeeper is asked to care without egocentricity, without grasping, without control, and perhaps even without emotional investment. "Real giving is essentially dark," writes the commentator. "This is the 'going beyond' of which Albert speaks, a desert of love, a night of trust."[1]

The Presence whom Carmelites have been contemplating for almost eight hundred years is a night that guides, an absence that reveals, a flame that heals. The Carmelite tradition offers a language for the soul helping to disclose this Presence deep within our lives. It is a language, ultimately, of attentive stillness, awaiting the lover's approach. This Carmelite way, born of the attempt to live in allegiance to Jesus Christ, is an ancient path for today's pilgrim.

NOTES

1. Kees Waaijman, O. Carm., "Carmelite Identity from the Perspective of the Rule," in *The Carmelite Family* (Melbourne: Carmelite Communications, 1994), 50.

Appendix

THE RULE OF CARMEL

(The rule of St. Albert given between 1206 and 1214)

Note: For the purpose of comparison, changes in St. Albert's original rule made by Pope Innocent IV in 1247 are indicated by (Inn.). Where this occurred, Albert's original rule is indicated by (Alb.).[1]

Introduction

Albert, called by God's favor to be Patriarch of the church of Jerusalem, bids health in the Lord and the blessing of the Holy Spirit to his beloved sons in Christ, B. and the other hermits under obedience to him who live near the spring on Mount Carmel.

Many and varied are the ways in which our saintly forefathers laid down how everyone whatever his station or the kind of religious observance he has chosen, should live a life of allegiance to Jesus Christ–how, pure in heart and stout in conscience, he must be unswerving in the service of his Master. It is to me, however, that you have come for a rule of life in keeping with your avowed purpose, a rule you may hold fast to henceforward; and therefore:

Chapter One

The first thing I require is for you to have a prior, one of yourselves, who is to be chosen for the office by common consent, or that of the greater or maturer part of you. Each of the others must promise him obedience—of which, once promised, he must try to make his deeds the true reflection—(Inn.) and also chastity and the renunciation of ownership.

Chapter Two

(Inn.) If the prior and the brothers see fit, you may have foundations in solitary places or where you are given a site that is suitable and convenient for the observance proper to your Order.

Chapter Three

Next, each one of you is to have a separate cell, situated as the lie of the land you propose to occupy may dictate, and allotted by disposition of the prior with agreement of the other brothers, or the more mature among them.

Chapter Four

(Inn.) However, you are to eat whatever may have been given you in a common refectory, listening together meanwhile to a reading from Holy Scripture where that can be done without difficulty.

Chapter Five

None of the brothers is to occupy a cell other than that allotted to him or to exchange cells with another, without leave of whoever is prior at the time.

Chapter Six

The prior's cell should stand near the entrance to your property, so that he may be the first to meet those who approach, and whatever has to be done in consequence may all be carried out as he may decide and order.

Chapter Seven

Each one of you is to stay in his cell or nearby, pondering the Lord's law day and night and keeping watch at his prayers unless attending to some other duty.

Chapter Eight

(Alb.) Those who know their letters, and how to read the psalms, should, for each of the hours, say those our holy forefathers laid down and the approved custom of the Church appoints for that hour. Those who do not know their letters must say 25 Our Fathers for the night office, except on Sundays and solemnities when that number is to be doubled so that the Our Father is said 50 times; the same prayer must be said seven times in the morning in the place of Lauds, and seven times too for each of the other hours, except for Vespers when it must be said 15 times.

(Inn.) Those who know how to say the canonical hours with those in Orders should do so, in the way those holy forefathers of ours laid down, and according to the Church's approved custom. Those who do not know the hours must say 25 Our Fathers for the night office, except on Sundays and solemnities when that number is to be doubled so that the Our Father is said 50 times; the same prayer must be said seven times in the morning place of Lauds, and seven times too for each of the other hours except for vespers when it must be said 15 times.

Chapter Nine

(Alb.) None of the brothers must lay claim to anything as his own, but your property is to be held in common; and of such things as the Lord may have given you each is to receive from the prior–that is the man he appoints for the purpose–whatever befits his age and needs. However, as I have said, each one of you is to stay in his own allotted cell, and live, by himself, on what is given out to him.

(Inn.) None of the brothers is to lay claim to anything as his own, but you are to possess everything in common; and each is to receive from the prior—that is the brother he appoints for the purpose—whatever befits his age and needs. (Inn.) You may have as many asses and mules as you need, however, and may keep a certain amount of livestock or poultry.

Chapter Ten

An oratory should be built as conveniently as possible among the cells, where, if it can be done without difficulty, you are to gather each morning to hear Mass.

Chapter Eleven

On Sundays too, or other days if necessary, you should discuss matters of discipline and your spiritual welfare; and on this occasion indiscretions and failings of the brothers, if any be found at fault, should be lovingly corrected.

Chapter Twelve

You are to fast every day, except Sundays, from the feast of the Exaltation of the Holy Cross until Easter Day, unless bodily sickness or feebleness, or some other good reason, demand a dispensation from the fast; for necessity overrides every law.

Chapter Thirteen

(Alb.) You are always to abstain from meat, unless it has to be eaten as a remedy for sickness or great feebleness.

(Inn.) You are to abstain from meat, except as a remedy for

sickness or feebleness. But as, when you are on a journey, you more often than not have to beg your way; outside your own houses you may eat foodstuffs that have been cooked with meat, so as to avoid giving trouble to your hosts. At sea, however, meat may be eaten.

Chapter Fourteen

Since man's life on earth is a time of trial, and all who live devotedly in Christ must undergo persecution, and the devil your foe is on the prowl like a roaring lion looking for prey to devour, you must use every care to clothe yourselves in God's armor so that you may be ready to withstand the enemy's ambush. Your loins are to be girt with chastity, your breast fortified by holy meditations, for, as Scripture has it, holy meditation will save you. Put on holiness as your breastplate, and it will enable you to love the Lord your God with all your heart and soul and strength, and your neighbor as yourself. Faith must be your shield on all occasions, and with it you will be able to quench all the flaming missiles of the wicked one; there can be no pleasing God without faith; (and the victory lies in your faith). On your head set the helmet of salvation and so be sure of deliverance by our only Savior, who sets his own free from their sins. The sword of the spirit, the word of God, must abound in your mouths and hearts. Let all you do have the Lord's word for accompaniment.

Chapter Fifteen

You must give yourselves to work of some kind, so that the devil may always find you busy; no idleness on your part must give him a chance to pierce the defenses of your souls. In this respect you have both the teaching and the example of St. Paul the Apostle, into whose mouth Christ put his own words. God made him preacher and teacher of faith and truth to the nations; with him as your leader you cannot go astray. We live among you, he said, laboring and weary, toiling night and day so as not to be a burden to any of you; not because we have no power to do otherwise but so as to give you, in our own selves, an example you might imitate. For the charge we gave you when we were with you was this: that whoever is not willing to work should not be allowed to eat either. For we have heard that there are certain restless idlers among you. We charge people of this kind, and implore them in the name of our Lord Jesus Christ, that they earn their own bread by silent toil. This is the way of holiness and goodness; see that you follow it.

Chapter Sixteen

The Apostle would have us keep silence, for in silence he tells us to work. As the prophet also makes known to us: Silence is the way to foster holiness. Elsewhere he says: Your strength will lie in silence and hope. (Alb.) For this reason I lay down that you are to keep silence from Vespers until Terce the next day, unless some necessary or some good reason, or the prior's permission, should break the silence. (Inn.) For this reason I lay down that you are to keep silence from after Compline until after Prime the next day. At other times, although you need not keep silence so strictly, be careful not to indulge in a great deal of talk, for, as Scripture has it—and experience teaches us no less—sin will not be wanting where there is much talk, and he who is careless in speech will come to harm; and elsewhere: The use of many words brings harm to the speaker's soul. And Our Lord says in the Gospel: Every rash word uttered will have to be accounted for on Judgment Day. Make a balance then, each of you, to weigh his words in; keep a tight rein on your mouths, lest you should stumble and fall in speech, and your fall be irreparable and prove mortal. Like the Prophet, watch your step lest your tongue give offense, and employ every care in keeping silent, which is the way to foster holiness.

Chapter Seventeen

You, brother B., and whoever may succeed you as prior, must always keep in mind and put into practice what our Lord said in the Gospel: Whoever has a mind to become a leader among you must make himself servant to the rest, and whichever of you would be first must become your bondsman.

Chapter Eighteen

You other brothers too, hold your prior in humble reverence, your minds not on him but on Christ who has placed him over you, and who, to those who rule the churches, addressed the words: Whoever pays you heed pays heed to me, and whoever treats you with dishonor dishonors me; if you remain so minded you will not be found guilty of contempt, but will merit life eternal as fit reward for your obedience.

Here then are a few points I have written down to provide you with a standard of conduct to live up to; but our Lord, at his Second Coming will reward anyone who does more than he is obliged to do. See that the bond of common sense is the guide of the virtues.[2]

---

1. Translation by Bede Edwards, OCD, in *The Rule of Saint Albert* (London: Aylesford and Kensington, 1973), 79–93. The original rule had no divisions. Eighteen chapters have been the traditional divisions since 1586.

2. A new translation of the rule, in places closer to the original Latin text, has been completed by Paul Chandler, O. Carm. He translated these last sentences of the rule: "We have written these things briefly for you, thus providing a formula for your way of life, according to which you are to live. Should anyone do more than prescribed, the Lord himself, when he returns, will reward him. Use discernment, however, the guide of the virtues."

Selected Bibliography

Chandler, Paul, O. Carm., ed. *A Journey with Elijah*. Rome: Casa Editrice Institutum Carmelitanum, 1991.

Cicconetti, Carlo, O. Carm. *The Rule of Carmel*. Trans. Gabriel Pausback, O. Carm. Ed. Paul Hoban, O. Carm. Darien, IL.: Carmelite Spiritual Center, 1984.

The Collected Works of St. John of the Cross. Trans. Kieran Kavanaugh, O.C.D., and Otilio Rodriguez, O.C.D. Washington, D.C.: ICS Publications, 1991.

The Collected Works of St. Teresa of Avila. 3 vols. Trans. Kieran Kavanaugh, O.C.D., and Otilio Rodriguez, O.C.D. Washington, D.C.: ICS Publications, 1976–1985.

Egan, Keith. "Carmelite Spirituality," in *The New Dictionary of Catholic Spirituality*. Collegeville: The Liturgical Press, 1993.

Friedman, Elias. *The Latin Hermits of Mount Carmel*. Rome: Institutum Historicum Teresianum, 1979.

Mulhall, Michael, O. Carm., ed. *Albert's Way*. Rome: Institutum Carmelitanum, 1989.

Ruiz, Federico, O.C.D., ed. *God Speaks in the Night*. Washington, D.C.: ICS Publications, 1991.

Slattery, Peter. *The Springs of Carmel*. New York: Alba House, 1991.

Smet, Joachim, O. Carm. *The Carmelites*, 4 vols. Darien, IL.: Carmelite Spiritual Center, 1976–1988.

———. *Cloistered Carmel*. Rome: Institutum Carmelitanum, 1986.

Staring, Adrianus, O. Carm., ed. *Medieval Carmelite Heritage*. Rome: Institutum Carmelitanum, 1989.

Thérèse of Lisieux, St. *Story of a Soul*. Trans. and ed. John Clarke, O.C.D. Washington, D.C.: ICS Publications, 1975.

Williams, Rowan. *Teresa of Avila*. Harrisburg, PA.: Morehouse Publishing, 1991.

Index